THE DUCHESS OF JERMYN STREET

Daphne Fielding

The Duchess of
Jermyn Street

The Life and Good Times of
ROSA LEWIS
of the Cavendish Hotel

Futura Publications Limited
A Futura Book

A Futura Book

First published in Great Britain in 1964
by Eyre & Spottiswoode (Publishers) Ltd

First Futura Publications edition 1976

Copyright © 1964 Daphne Fielding

ISBN 0 8600 7435 8
Printed in Great Britain by
Hazell Watson & Viney Ltd
Aylesbury, Bucks

Futura Publications Limited
110 Warner Road,
Camberwell, London SE5

Preface

Many attempts were made during her long life to portray the character of Rosa Lewis. She captivated the imagination and curiosity of Londoners – transient or permanent – of many kinds. It was most desirable that a definitive study should be made before she passed into legend. Here it is, written by one who knew her well, enjoyed her confidence, understood her idiosyncrasies and had also the skill and patience to investigate the authentic sources.

This is the portrait of an era as well as of one of its protagonists.

My own connexion with Rosa was tenuous. I first met her at about the same time as Mrs Fielding. I had not then started on the profession she abhorred. I was introduced into the Cavendish by Mr Alastair Graham, who is mentioned in this book, and welcomed as one of the moneyless young men whose wine was charged to the bills of older and richer customers. Five years later I was expelled with the words: 'Take your arse out of my chair, Lulu Walters-Waugh' (Rosa was at the time engaged in a row with a contemporary of mine named Lulu Welch. She liked, as Mrs Fielding points out, to confuse names.) Our brief acquaintance was largely vicarious. I stayed at the Cavendish once and spent several jolly evenings there, but I was never an habitué; I was seldom in London and the character I drew from her in my second novel was mostly derived at second hand from the anecdotes and imitations of my friends. Thus, when it was suggested that I should write her life, I knew I was incapable. Mrs Fielding, as will be seen in the following pages, was the obvious person to take it on.

She has succeeded as no one else could. It was a task of the utmost difficulty. We are nearing the centenary of Rosa's birth. Legends, which she did little to dissipate, proliferated about her early years and the fascination of this book lies almost as much in the falsehoods that are exposed as in the truths which research has established. There was the further difficulty that Rosa excelled in the two *métiers* in which triumph is most transient and most incommunicable. She was a great cook in the classic tradition and she was a great cockney clown. There are few people now alive who tasted her quail pudding. Those now in middle age knew her as a richly comic entertainer whose jokes, lacking her timing and tone of voice, tend to vanish when set down in print.

Mrs Fielding, it seems to me, has been brilliantly successful both in evoking the Edwardian era before her own birth, when Rosa was working strenuously to achieve her unique position, and in reporting the later years which she knew so intimately, when Rosa had abandoned the kitchen and was the sharp, garrulous hostess to a diverse, but never dull, company. Mrs Fielding gives us the picture of two ages, one created in the imagination, one keenly observed; more than this she gives the first full, true portrait of a warm-hearted, comic and totally original woman.

EVELYN WAUGH

Acknowledgements

My most grateful thanks are due to Miss Edith Jeffery, who, in spite of her reluctance to encourage anything to be written about her beloved Rosa, finally allowed me to go through her albums and provided photographs and menus. But never for a moment would she betray her friend's confidences. Whenever I tried to tap Rosa's secrets she closed like a clam.

At the very outset I was faced with a problem of research. So many people who might have been sources of information have died: others were cagey. But Sir Shane Leslie had pity on my thirst and allowed me to dip deep into the well of his unfailing memory. Evelyn Waugh shone guiding lights, Joseph Bryan III sent me his 'profile' of Rosa published in the *New Yorker* in 1933 and opened up new channels. The late Sir Timothy Eden allowed me to include his father's letters. 'If he does not approve you will hear about it at the last trump,' he added. To all these I offer my most sincere thanks. I also benefited from George Kinnaird's experience in publishing which contributed to the planning of this book. Many people were very helpful in answering my inquiries and providing me with valuable information, especially the following:
Sir Philip Magnus Alcroft, the Honorable Robert Coe, Daniel Caulkins, Lady Kathleen Curzon Herrick, Sir Michael Duff, Sir Philip Dunn, Viscountess Gage, Alistair Graham, Mark Ogilvie Grant, Captain Kenyon Goode, the late Aldous Huxley, Mr Jones of Laurie and Jones, Lord Kinross, Lord Lovat, George Millar, Robin McDouall, Jack Pringle, Mrs Anne Ross, Sir Osbert Sitwell, Alexander Sedgwick, Muriel

Segal, Mrs Peter Thursby, David Tennant, Iris Tree, Lady Moorea Wyatt, Lothar Wolff.

I must also acknowledge the following authors and publishers who gave permission for me to quote from the works mentioned: Shane Leslie and Chatto & Windus Ltd for excerpts from *The Anglo-Catholic* by Shane Leslie; Cassell & Co. Ltd for excerpts from Lord Ribblesdale's *Impressions and Memories;* Michael Harrison and Peter Davies for excerpts from *Rosa* by Michael Harrison; William Heinemann Ltd for excerpts from *A Generation Missing* by Carroll Carstairs; Cornelia Otis Skinner and Michael Joseph Ltd for a quotation from *Elegant Wits and Grand Horizontals* by Cornelia Otis Skinner; the *Sunday Telegraph* and Pauline Massingham for excerpts from her article on Rosa Lewis; the *Daily Telegraph* for an excerpt from their report on a Foreign Office banquet which Rosa organized in 1909; Colliers for an excerpt from an article by Walter Davenport; the *New York Times* for excerpts from an interview with Rosa Lewis; the *Evening Standard* for an extract from Maureen Cleave's article on the Cavendish.

And finally I thank my husband, Xan Fielding, who in the midst of his own literary work gave me constructive criticism and help.

DAPHNE FIELDING
Vale de Lobos
Portugal

to Edith with love

Chapter One

It was a sad day of rain on Wednesday, December 23rd, 1952. A cold wind blew down Jermyn Street as the taxis honked and tooted past the Cavendish Hotel. Inside the Georgian church of St James's, Piccadilly, the coffin of Mrs Rosa Lewis rested in the broad aisle. It was covered with the flowers she loved the most: roses, carnations, mimosa, gardenias and orchids. There was not room for them all, since four carts had been piled high with these last votive offerings. In the distance the plaintive voice of a barrel-organ churned out a hackneyed song of joy and regret.

The church was crowded with mourners as her old friend and sometime rival, Archdeacon Lambert, took the funeral service. Over the years he had come to look like one of the pelicans in St James's Park, just round the corner. Did he perhaps remember how some of his parishioners had lingered at the Cavendish and missed Matins of a Sunday?

It was a curiously assorted congregation, steeped in mink and funeral hush, for Mrs Lewis had known princes and paupers, and ladies of fashion and ladies of the town. Many of her clients had been christened in St James's; some of them were buried there. Most of those who had come to honour her cherished memories of times spent in her famous establishment opposite, where laughter bubbled like the ever-flowing champagne. Indeed Jermyn Street was not unlike the Sunday-school illustration of the 'Broad and Narrow Way', with the church on the one side and the Cavendish on the other.

The voices join in the hymn 'Rock of Ages', as the coffin is carried out of the church.

Edith Jeffrey, her devoted friend for forty years, looks like a small migratory bird stranded companionless upon some alien shore. She is wearing Rosa's fur coat and toque, which are too big for her frail body. Her eyes are red from weeping and hazy with tears. 'She was such a great lady,' she sighs. 'Funerals seem dreadful, don't they?'

Who was this legendary old lady, Rosa Lewis? The old lady who was so often seen standing at the entrance of her famous hotel in Jermyn Street, her white hair impeccably waved in the old-fashioned manner, with curling-tongs, by her hairdresser who attended her daily; her nails freshly manicured, but her face innocent of make-up?

She dressed in a style of her own, outside fashion. Her trailing coat and skirt were made from the very best material, cut many years ago by Busvine, tailor by royal appointment to Queen Mary. Around her neck she always wore, scarfwise, a man's white cambric handkerchief. Against her knees clanked a long string of amber beads reminiscent of a muff-chain. Standing in the front porch with an old white Aberdeen terrier at her heels she would 'scan-the-trott' imperiously, raising a goblet of champagne in recognition of passers-by. She looked like a queen and could swear like a cook, which indeed she was. In fact today there is hardly a figure in *Debrett* who will not tell you that Rosa Lewis cooked for his grandmother, as she did for mine, Mrs Harry McCalmont, whenever she entertained Edward VII (then Prince of Wales) at Chieveley Park, Newmarket.

Rosa knew me first when I was small enough to be used, so it is said, as a missile, like Punch and Judy's baby, in the violent quarrels between my father and mother. She admired my beautiful bolting mother, Barbara Fanning, who was divorced from my father when I was 4 years old, after leaving him for a man who, she found out too late, was already married; on discovering this she took refuge at the Cavendish and, according to Rosa, my mother then pelted him with the jewels he had given her.

Rosa told me this story in 1926, when Lord Charles Cavendish took me to make a clandestine call on her at the hotel, which was out of bounds to my débutante world. I was spellbound by this account, since throughout my childhood no one would tell me anything about my mother, for mention even of her name was forbidden, and I had romanticized her from the vague memory I cherished of a laughing golden corn-goddess.

It soon became clear to my young mind that the reason both my grandmothers, as well as my father and my more broadminded stepmother, disapproved of the Cavendish was that Mrs Lewis knew much too much about their generation, some of whom seemed to have left skeletons in her wardrobes which they preferred to forget. If she could be persuaded to talk over a glass of champagne there was much to be learnt, and her disclosures made one's relations far more interesting; it was particularly fascinating that she knew who really were the fathers of one's friends.

Through the big double doors of the Cavendish, painted Guardi green,† past the porch where an enormous hooded leather chair stood like a monument, I found an Alice-in-Wonderland, Through-the-Looking-Glass world that enchanted me, where the faster one ran the more one stayed in the same place – at the Cavendish. Here Rosa reigned, both as Red Queen and White Queen, with her 'off with his head' manner

† Lord Ribblesdale's favourite colour.

to anyone she didn't like and her trailing scarf slipping off her shoulders. She was also the Duchess, with a background of pig-and-pepper kitchen. Tweedledees and Tweedledums had fought their battles at the Cavendish, and the place was chock-a-block with Mad Hatters: there was even one who used to stir butter into his red wine. The clients were often caught in Anglo-Saxon attitudes, and a character called 'Froggy' used to live there who wasn't a frog footman.

When I first met Rosa, the legend was that she had been the mistress of Edward VII, and Lord Ribblesdale's name was also linked with hers; but that was only what people said. Rosa herself neither confirmed nor denied these rumours. She knew just how to throw in a red herring to change a conversation, and she never discussed her secret heart.

It was sometimes her pleasure to leave her birth shrouded in mystery, and, to a new acquaintance, she might have arrived in a magic circle with those other Rhinemaidens, descending on her favourite market at Covent Garden instead of the Opera House. She certainly had the stature and vitality of those resonant beauties.

In the days when the Cavendish was on the highest crest of the wave, Rosa would amuse herself by hinting to her most favoured clients that her birth had been in France, in the very grandest circumstances, even if the blankets had got a bit muddled in the laundry. The very fact that the hotel billheads announced that in this establishment French, German, and Spanish were spoken smacked of upper-crust cosmopolitania, and was one in the eye for Frau Sacher, her rival in Vienna, into whose famous café visiting royalty and the smart *demi-monde* crowded to eat her renowned *Sachertorte*.

As Rosa swept regally down the corridors of her elegant hotel, trailing clouds of glory, she evoked visionary fountains and ephemeral châteaux. On the other hand, when she chose to stamp her foot in a moment of anger and give the rough side of her tongue to an erring waiter, one could well imagine that her ancestors, if French they were, would have been found knitting on the wrong side both of the guillotine and the blanket. But Rosa had no French blood. Her great-great-grandmother, Maria Sanchez, was Spanish: a capable woman who carried on her husband's business after his death, and whose great-great-grand-daughter certainly possessed the pride and dash of the Spanish temper.

The truth is Rosa was neither Rhinemaiden, nor Royal, nor even French, but a genuine cockney. Her speech confirmed this, but was in no way unattractive; in fact it was a part of her charm since it was robust and characteristic. When she spoke one was reminded of that song of Elsie Janis's, 'When she dropped her H's it made you raise your I's'.

A recent article in the *Sunday Telegraph* by Pauline Massingham accurately describes Rosa's manner of talking:

> "'Vrilda-a!'
>
> 'I can hear her now as I write.
>
> 'My name in those days was Vilda, but Rosa always mispronounced it. Although she had been the friend of kings and queens and dukes and duchesses, and lords and ladies, she often still spoke in the clipped accents of her youth. Perhaps it was a part of her indomitable independence. Her cockney was of a kind that is rarely heard today. Although she scattered H's wherever she went, her great peculiarity was that she introduced an R between a consonant and a vowel. So she said Vrilda for Vilda. She said bralcony for balcony. When she called for Moon, the faithful white-haired porter, she often shouted "Mroon!"'

17

Rosa was not unlike Nell Gwynn, whom she resembled in her compassion, common sense and wit, in her determination and vitality, and above all in her robust use of the King's English. It was Nell, who, when the King called to see her and asked after the children, bawled out as their eldest son passed the door, 'Come here, you little bastard, and speak to your father.' Charles, outraged, said with some pomposity, 'How dare you call my son a bastard?' Whereupon Nell replied, 'And what else, Sire, can I call him?' Thus Nell got her way and had the dukedom of St Albans added to her heritage.

Her approach to life had much in common with Rosa's: a blend of dignity and a genius for marrying her natural wit to her God-given looks, and so achieving the best for all in the best of all possible worlds. Indeed when Nell Gwynn had that unfortunate contretemps in the city of London and her gilded coach was mobbed by an angry crowd who had mistaken it for Louise de Kéroualle's it might have been Rosa who leant out of the window and said, 'Good people, I am the Protestant whore.'

To solve the legend of this remarkable woman we must go back to September 27th, 1867, when Rosa Ovenden was born in a cottage at Grange Road, Leyton. Leyton is now a suburb of London, but in those days it was a small village lying along the road which joins Bethnal Green with Waltham Cross. Her parents, William and Eliza Ovenden, had nine children and Rosa was the fifth. In spite of what must have been very overcrowded living quarters, these children had a strong life-force; well fed and cared for, they all survived – an unusual phenomenon in Victorian days.

William Ovenden was a watchmaker, and in order to make more money to feed his growing family, he also entered into partnership with his brother, who had a prosperous undertaker's business at Islington, and started a branch office in Ley-ton. This proved a success and a few years later he was able to buy the two cottages next to the one in which Rosa had been born.

Rosa's mother, Eliza Cannon, was the daughter of a retired jeweller, one of a family of artisans whose origins have recently been traced by that well known expert on London, Michael Harrison. 'The Cannons were established in the cities of Lon-don and Westminster as early as the reign of Elizabeth I, several being described as "gentlemen" in the marriage regis-ters of the various London parishes which in those days would imply that they were "gentlemen of coat armour" entitled to sport armorial bearings.'†

Rosa's maternal great-great-uncle, Richard Cannon, was patronized by the Prince Regent. The son of a papier-mâché merchant, he was educated at a public school and went to a university. He became a clerk at the Horse Guards, and soon rose to the position of first clerk in charge of regimental records. Through the Prince Regent's passion for all things military, particularly uniforms, a professional friendship flourished between these two. Thanks to this, Richard Cannon was able to put in a good word for his family, who were in many branches of trade.

The firm of Cannon & Buzzard were commissioned to supply the Prince both at Carlton House Terrace and the Pavilion, and were given a royal warrant as 'purveyors' to the Prince's and King's household. In the reign of William IV, Richard Cannon had become principal clerk in the department of the Adjutant-General. He retired in 1854 on a full salary, which in those days would be comparable with a taxed income of £8,000 today.

† Michael Harrison, *Rosa*.

It was this great-great-uncle of Rosa's who was able to use his influence to secure a commission for the jewellers in his family to assist in the making of Queen Victoria's Coronation crown.

All the Ovenden children were eventually baptized, but for convenience their parents seemed to have adopted the practice of christening them in batches, as though they were cakes to be baked, and on June 27th, 1869, Rosa was christened in the parish church of St Mary-the-Virgin at the same time as her sister Lucy and brother Frederick. According to Michael Harrison, Rosa was duly confirmed as a child, but in fact this ceremony was omitted at the time and was not to be performed until after she was 80. Throughout her life she was a church-goer, and her religion remained steadfast.

She must have been an exceptionally lovely girl, tall and well made, her mass of silky dark-brown hair contrasting with her deeply set forget-me-not blue eyes. One can see in her photo-graphs the strength and beauty of her bone structure, the high cheek-bones and characteristic well-moulded chin, its firmness tempered by a roguish rounded nose and a laughing mouth. Her brilliant high colouring reminded one of Sargent's picture 'Carnation, Lilly, Lilly, Rose'. How Renoir would have been enchanted by that fabulous skin of hers which took the light! She held herself proudly and walked with an air, full of the vitality which sprang joyously from youthful strength and health and shone in the radiance of her smile.

She was born with an independent spirit and her earliest memory was that of making up her mind to escape from home as soon as she could. No doubt the fact of being one of such a large family contributed to the urge and determination to leave the crowded nest and fly towards broader horizons.

She went to the Board School at Church Road, Leyton,

when she was 8 years old, her parents paying the nominal penny a week, but after four years her education ended abruptly. She was now considered old enough to go out to work and make the customary contribution from her wages to her parents.

Her brown hair still hung down her back when she took a post as general servant to Mr and Mrs Ralph Musgrave, at 3 Myrtle Villas, where she was paid a shilling a week and her keep. Mrs Musgrave permitted her to wear her hair in a long plait, but insisted on the lengthening of her skirts and also provided her with tight shoes which squeezed her growing feet. Poor child! She must have been like a young colt, shod for the first time, and forced between the shafts.

The little maid of all work began her household chores at 5.30 a.m. in the winter, and the dreary round was not over until nine o'clock at night, when she climbed into her narrow iron bedstead, and, tired as she was, read by candlelight all the old newspapers which were put aside for lighting the fires. (Who could have believed that one day the name of this Cinderella figure would carry front-page news-value?) Reading accounts of Court balls, dinners, garden parties, race meetings and shoots, she fell asleep to dream of royalty and other nobs.

After four years of drab duties at 3 Myrtle Villas she told the surprised Mrs Musgrave that she wished to leave at the end of the month. This move met with her parents' disapproval, but she remained adamant in the face of persuasion and threats and left this first post of hers with an excellent reference. She had reached a cross-roads in her young life, and one of her favourite stories later was of the decision with which she was then faced.

In those days there were two obvious careers open to a good-looking girl who had to earn a living – that of a prostitute or a domestic servant. Rosa decided to plump for the latter and to concentrate on cooking, for which she already showed some aptitude; but she wanted to serve the kind of people she read about in the Court circulars of the *Morning Post* and magazines like *Modern Society*. This dazzling world fascinated her and she knew all the names of the fashionable by heart.

Our Cinderella's longing for an escutcheoned background of crowns and strawberry leaves was soon to be gratified, for a lucky star had appeared on her horizon, a star which was to lead her towards the very highest French society. Through the good graces of her uncle, who was a friend of the Comtesse de Paris's chef at Sheen House, Mortlake, she obtained a post as an under kitchen-maid with a wage of 12s. 6d. a week. For many months her sole job was the scrubbing of kitchen floors, but 16-year-old Rosa was so happy that she might have been scrubbing the floors of Heaven, for even though the Comte de Paris was exiled he was heir to the throne of France.

Chapter Two

Rosa Ovenden was not to remain scrubbing floors for long. Soon she was allowed to do the washing up, for it had been noticed that she was careful and had a light touch with china. Her love of beautiful objects began to burgeon over the soap-suds as she washed the magnificent Sévres dinner service, and although she performed her work quickly and deftly, she wove day-dreams round the coroneted plates rimmed with royal blue and gold and decorated with the lilies of St Louis.

She was the only English person in the kitchen at Sheen House, but her native wit enabled her to pick up sufficient French to understand what was required of her. It must have been at this time that she began to assimilate the faultless French which she later used in her menus.

The little English girl was teased by her colleagues but she took it all in good part. One can imagine a saucy *sous-chef* giving Rosa's silky brown plait a provocative tug as he winked at her passing by, '*Et alors, queue de vache*', and Rosa with a laugh picking up a couple of wooden spoons, holding them to her forehead as she tossed her head in imitation of a cow, then hurrying on to the scullery with a swish of her pigtail.

Her next step up was being allowed to gut the poultry and game – a task to which she added a special refinement by sewing up the incisions neatly with a needle and thread. From this she was promoted to making the coffee and tea.

Rosa always spoke of the Comtesse de Paris with the greatest respect: throughout her life this woman remained one of her heroines. She was not a beauty, although she must have had a striking presence. She had fine dark eyes and a mass of black hair, which she dressed in the style of the Empress Eugénie. Her eyebrows were strongly marked over slightly drooping eyelids. One imagines, from her photographs, a faint moustache. Rosa described her as being very masculine. She was a first-rate horsewoman, an excellent shot and enjoyed smoking a cigar.

The children of the Comte and Comtesse de Paris were carefully brought up and disciplined, their mother being very exacting as to appearance, manners and deportment. She often visited the kitchen on her way out riding, and if she noticed a kitchen-maid holding herself badly she would give her a sharp slap across the shoulders with her riding-whip, saying, *'Tiens-toi droit, mon enfant.'* Her own children received the same treatment. She was punctual to a point; a quality which young Rosa found admirable. In after years she would describe how the Comtesse de Paris was so methodical that she always put on her chemise at precisely the same time every day.

Catching fleeting glimpses of the children of the house, Rosa's lively imagination played round them: hers was never a jealous nature and she did not envy them. She particularly admired Princesse Amélie, the future Queen of Portugal, because she had acquired a number of medical degrees. She was also enamoured of the eldest son, the Duc d'Orléans, renowned in his heyday as a ladies' man.

Years later, when Rosa was in her middle age, Sir Osbert Sitwell asked her if she had ever fallen in love at first sight. 'Of course,' was the emphatic reply. 'And with whom?' inquired Sir Osbert. 'With the Duke of Orleans when he walked into the kitchen as I was making toast.' 'And what did you do?' 'Burnt the toast, of course!'

So Rosa's progress continued. From toast-making she was promoted to dealing with the vegetables (a branch of cooking in which she always excelled) and all the time she was watching and learning, missing nothing as she stored away her knowledge like a squirrel building up its winter cache of nuts.

Throughout the time she was in service to the Comte and Comtesse de Paris she sent a part of her earnings back home. She had never seen so much money before. Starting with 12s. 6d. a week, her wages must have been raised as she performed more responsible jobs, and besides, there were sometimes small presents of money that also came her way. She never spent much upon herself and was always ready to lend or give away her last penny.

The Comte and Comtesse de Paris entertained a great deal. The Prince of Wales often came to Sheen House, and there is a charming story about Rosa's first meeting with him. At the end of a dinner-party it was suggested that the guests sang 'God bless the Prince of Wales' but there was no piano in the room, and, as so often happens when voices join in impromptu singing, a leader was needed. 'There's a girl in the kitchen who is always singing,' someone volunteered. 'Why not ask her up? She's got a good strong voice.' The girl was summoned.

She was pretty Rosa Ovenden of the forget-me-not blue eyes. 'Oh yes, I can sing loud enough,' she said, 'but I'm not always in tune,' and without a trace of coyness she led off with her strong young voice and all the nobs of the Prince of Wales's set followed her in the song. Afterwards she was presented to the Prince, who complimented her on the excellence of the ptarmigan pie. She dropped a curtsy and laughed as she said, 'The chef makes the pies, sir, I just take the innards out of the birds, sir,' whereupon the Prince patted her on the shoulder and pulled out the little purse full of sovereigns that he kept ready for gifts.

Another version of the story, reputedly from Rosa's own lips, is that she was presented to the Prince after he had commented on the excellence of the plain but beautifully cooked meal of boiled broad beans with bacon and parsley sauce which she had prepared in the chef's absence. On this occasion he presented her with a gold sovereign, making a royal quip, 'A sovereign, my dear, from your future sovereign.'

Inevitably the looks of the pretty, lively English girl did not pass unnoticed in this Latin household. There were times when she was nervous as to Froggies who would a-wooing go, and so she used to barricade her bedroom door with furniture. But a wily Greek, Prince Ypsilanti, the Minister to King George of the Hellenes and a renowned roué, slipped into her bedroom one night before she came up from the kitchen. Rosa found him waiting, fully confident, wearing what she described as 'very tight pyjamas'. Keeping her head, she threatened to scream at the top of her robust young lungs. 'I don't care who you are,' she said, stamping her foot, 'but I'll tell you straight that I'm worth just as much to my parents as you are to yours, and probably a good sight more. If you lay a finger on me I'll go straight and tell the Countess.' The middle-aged satyr removed himself as fast as 'the very tight pyjamas' would permit.

Rosa Ovenden seems to have been shared among other members of the Orléans family, for she was lent, with the reputation of a highly competent kitchen-maid, to the Comte de Paris's uncle, the Duc d'Aumale, who was the son of Louis Philippe and the acknowledged leader of *le gratin*, the highest of French society. His château at Chantilly was like the illustration of a fairy-story castle, surrounded by a moat enclosing formal gardens. In the parklands beyond were lakes and waterfalls. Young

Rosa must have walked through the woods, where paths were cut leading to hidden Greek temples, catching glimpses of marble statues between the trees. In the forest the Duc d'Aumale hunted the deer with his own pack of hounds, and the château had its private stables and race-course.

Here was a *grand seigneur* in every respect. A hero in the field of battle, Aumale had distinguished himself when the French were defeated at Sedan in the Franco-Prussian War. In Algeria he had led the Zouaves to victory. During the Second Empire he was exiled from France for twenty-two years, but with the overthrow of the Bonapartes he returned to command the army of the republic. After its defeat in 1879, he said, 'France is broken but the pieces are still good.'

Although a man of immense civilization and taste, he was before anything else a soldier. On first being gazetted as a sub-lieutenant he said, 'My only ambition is to be the forty-third Bourbon killed on the field of battle,' but this glorious fate was not to be his for he survived all his campaigns. In 1886 he was again exiled when all pretenders to the throne were banished; but when the *Institut de France* learned that he intended to leave Chantilly to them, he was welcomed back in the republic.

This many-faceted man was a great historian and among the books he wrote was a seven-volume opus on the lives of the Princes de Condé. He was also an art connoisseur and bibliophile and the possession of the Duc de Berry's illuminated *Book of Hours*, gave him exquisite pleasure. His wit remained blade-sharp until the end although he suffered acutely from gout. In his declining days he said of himself, 'As a young buck, I always had four supple members and one stiff one . . . now I have four stiff and one supple.'†

Rosa felt proud and privileged to be in the employ of a

† Cornelia Otis Skinner, *Elegant Wits and Grand Horizontals*.

great gentleman endowed with all the *panache* that she so admired, and her blue eyes widened with wonder as she listened to the gossip which bubbled round *le gratin*. She added to her inventory of names those of *grandes demi-mondaines* such as Léonide Leblanc (Aumale's most famous mistress), Cléo de Merode, Diane de Pougy and Caroline Otero. The gilded life of *la belle époque* seemed as distant as another planet from the suburban existence of Myrtle Villas. Young Rosa Ovenden had already journeyed a long, long way.

After a summer at Chantilly she returned to England in the autumn and, with the rest of the Comte de Paris's staff, went up north for the shooting season, where she gained more golden experience in the cooking of all kinds of game which was to become her *forte*. For a short time, until a suitable chef could be found for the Duc d'Orléans, who by then had moved into an establishment of his own at Sandhurst, she took complete charge of the kitchen there. But she no longer burnt the toast whenever the master of the house walked in.

By the time she returned to Sheen House, as head kitchen-maid, she was 20 years old and had been with the Comte and Comtesse de Paris four years. She had learnt that cooking was indeed an art, and one that was appreciated by her beloved aristocrats. Her instinct told her that she now held the key to patrician hearts and homes. Her ambition, as well as her sense of adventure, urged her to try her skill still farther afield. She had almost reached the top of the kitchen ladder in the Comte de Paris's household and could have stayed there indefinitely, but London challenged her. She had gained all the necessary experience and she was confident in her talent and capability. Throughout her life she retained this blessed spirit of confidence : it was the wind that blew her kite so high.

Her star had risen at precisely the right time, for food had never been so important in Society as it was with the Edwardians. People could climb into Society on the shoulders of a good cook. Rosa not only had talent and experience, she was also developing a keenly critical eye. To her mind the French chefs 'messed up' good food with all their sauces, and she thought the menus at Sheen House were not sufficiently varied; a special dish was ordered only when English royalty were guests. Economy was no doubt a necessity in this house of exiles, but stinting was something that Rosa could not tolerate. She felt sure there would be no scraping and paring once she was cooking for the swells in London.

In 1887 she therefore gave in her notice to the Comte de Paris's secretary. It was received with regret, and she was given an excellent reference.

Rosa did not make the mistake of rushing into a permanent place without very thorough consideration. She went home for a bit, but her own family life had never meant very much to her and it must have then seemed narrower than ever. To get away from it, she took a temporary place with a fussy old lady in Chester Square, who complained of Rosa's extravagance and interfered with her comings and goings, thinking her too young and good-looking to be given any liberty. Rosa did not wait long before giving in her notice, but when she did the old lady sent for Mr and Mrs Ovenden to fetch their daughter, since she feared it would be unsafe for her to travel alone. When her parents rang the back-door bell, Rosa walked out of the front door to seek another job on her own.

Luck was with her. She went to an agency, where she was told that Lady Randolph Churchill needed an occasional cook to replace her hard-worked chef on his days off.

Rosa knew all about Lady Randolph Churchill, having

followed each step of her course in the Society papers and magazines. She remembered that Jenny Jerome had been acclaimed as one of the prettiest American girls to storm London Society. She had cut Jenny's pictures out of a paper announcing her engagement to Lord Randolph and treasured a magazine photograph of a group taken at her wedding. Rosa always had heroines in her life: the Comtesse de Paris was the first one, but the most adored of all was Lady Randolph.

It is more than probable that the young Churchills were entertained by the Comte and Comtesse de Paris at Sheen House. They may have heard of the talented kitchen-maid who was able to replace the chef at a moment's notice. Lord Randolph was both a gourmet and a gourmand. It was said of him that he would rather eat a perfect dish of his favourite *oeufs brouillés aux truffes* than have a seat in the Cabinet.

Jenny Jerome's marriage was not a very happy one and she found a certain consolation in keeping open house for her friends. She was a hostess of taste and discrimination, taking infinite pains with the smallest details. The path of her entertaining was not always smooth and often there was trouble with the cooks. At one of the first dinner-parties she gave when she was newly married, her over-excited and absent-minded chef served the patties, which should have been for the entrée, floating in the soup, whereas the poached eggs intended for this purpose appeared ungarnished on a plate. (Perhaps these reminded some of the guests of Lord Randolph's eyes!)

We can be quite sure that Lady Randolph quickly engaged Rosa Ovenden on seeing her reference from the Comtesse de Paris.

The first meal that Rosa cooked for her new employer was an unqualified success. It was a big dinner-party, and Rosa performed wonders without making any fuss. Unlike poor Vatel, the highly-strung chef of the Prince de Condé who, when Louis XIV was dining at Chantilly, fell on his sword because the fish had not turned up in time,* Rosa never despaired in the face of disaster. She merely let off steam by swearing.

After she had cooked that first memorable dinner for her heroine, an arrangement was made with her to 'oblige' whenever the chef took his day off. Lady Randolph also recommended the new-found treasure to a few friends, but made it quite clear that she had first claim on the exceptionally talented young cook, who among her other qualifications was gaining a reputation as 'a card', her sayings being repeated round fashionable dining-tables. When things went wrong in a household she was able to change the tempo by raising a laugh with her lively quips, and if she was criticized she never shifted the blame on to anyone else: this remained one of her lifelong principles.

With so much to her credit there was now no need for her to take a permanent place: people were soon clamouring for her and, knowing her own worth, she charged through the nose. But although she was earning a great deal as an occasional cook, when her heroine offered her a post in a permanent capacity, she immediately accepted.

It was about this time, according to Mary Lawton,† that Rosa's cooking first came to the notice of the Prince of Wales. Although there had recently been very bad blood between H.R.H. and Lord Randolph – the latter's brother, Lord Blandford, had recently run off with Lady Aylesford who was married to one of the leading members of the Marlborough House set – the Prince had since forgiven the man he nicknamed

* This drastic action proved unnecessary since a few minutes after he died, the tide having turned, the fish was delivered.

† Mary Lawton, *A Queen of Cooks and Some Kings.*

'gooseberry-faced Churchill' and was once again willing to be his guest for the sake of the *beaux yeux* of his attractive wife whom he had admired since her débutante days.

No wonder, for Lady Randolph was a remarkable woman. In addition to her dark velvety beauty she had the intellectual attainments that were to be found in her sister, Lady Leslie. Before going on what she called in her memoirs 'a pilgrimage' to Bayreuth for a Wagner festival, she arranged a series of lectures on 'The Ring' at Lady Leslie's house. 'In order to familiarize us with the score, a German musician, a well-known exponent of the Art of Wagner, was pressed into service and he brought with him a lady who was to sing the different motifs.'

Lady Randolph must have been a hostess comparable, in later years, to Lady Cunard or Lady Colefax. She liked to entertain men of letters (something of a phenomenon in Edwardian days) and once had a sharp telegraphic passage of arms with Bernard Shaw after inviting him to lunch. His churlish answer to her read:

'Certainly not. What have I done to provoke such an attack on my well known habits?'†

Lady Randolph replied:

'Know nothing of your habits. Hope they are not as bad as your manners.'

For some time Lady Randolph and the Comtesse de Paris corresponded over '*La Ligue de la Rose*' which the latter had started to help restore the monarchy in France. This organization was intended to be a sister of the Primrose League, of which Lady Randolph was a leading figure, and the rose was adopted as its symbol. When Rosa was interviewed by Mary Lawton in the twenties, she apparently indulged in the fantasy

† George Bernard Shaw was a vegetarian.

that the new league was named after her because the Comtesse de Paris looked upon her as a mascot. One can only believe that this *folie de grandeur* arose from a momentary *folie de champagne*.

Apart from Rosa's admiration for Lady Randolph, she sympathized with her when she was treated badly by Lord Randolph. Rosa was a strong feminist. She knew that most of the money came from Jenny Jerome's dowry, and it shocked her to see Lord Randolph running up such huge gambling debts. She remembered, too, how he had behaved when Lady Randolph had had a bad fall while hunting with him in Leicestershire. Perhaps it was due to the shock of seeing his wife lying unconscious that his immediate reaction was to seize the flask from her saddle and drain it dry. As Lady Randolph neatly commented: 'I had the fall, he had the brandy.'

Throughout her life Rosa was amused by practical jokes, but she thought that Lady Blandford went a little too far when she put a celluloid baby doll under the silver cover of the breakfast dish which should have contained her husband's breakfast bacon and eggs, this underlining the fact that Lord Blandford had fathered a child by that forlorn and forsaken beauty, Lady Aylesford.

The Edwardian era was the heyday of the practical joke and what got back to the servants' hall via the valets and the ladies' maids must have mitigated the tedium of the scullery floor and the kitchen sink. At Rufford Abbey, for instance, one of the best shoots and most nobly haunted houses in England, Lord and Lady Saville unwisely opened their doors one season to a banished Russian Grand Duke. Rosa, who had been engaged as a temporary cook there, always remembered the consequences. The bangs that went off on the moors were nothing to the bangs in the bedrooms, with the crash of booby traps falling on guests' heads and the rattle of cotton-reels concealed in chamber-pots. The ghosts were not amused. But the servants were. As one of the footmen remarked to Rosa in tones of admiration: 'They say he's as mad as a hatter. He once had a chocolate *soufflé* put on a chair, then sat on it in his riding-breeches – right in the middle of one of them posh froggy cafés at Monte it was.' 'What's sauce for the goose is sauce for the gander,' Rosa retorted, 'but don't let me catch you, young Henry, sitting on one of our chocolate puddings.'

These high jinks were not confined to Russian Grand Dukes. The Prince of Wales himself still enjoyed a boyish prank although he was now 48. Even intellectual Lady Randolph indulged in these jokes, and at a dinner-party where the Prince and Princess of Wales were present she announced that she was wearing 'a Jubilee bustle' which played 'God Save the Queen' whenever she sat down. The source of the anthem proved to be a pint-sized A.D.C. hidden under her chair with a musical box which he turned at the appropriate moment.

Another prankster was the millionaire Jimmy White. To act as waiters at a stag dinner he once gave to other wealthy friends he engaged the Egbert Brothers who were a popular knock-about music-hall turn, granting them *carte blanche* to behave exactly as they did in their slapstick act. The guests were startled by piles of plates crashing round them, by rolls made of cement, by knives and forks which collapsed when put to use, by water squirting from the floral decorations and, at the bottom of the soup, rubber spiders and discarded sets of false teeth.

Edwardian young women were often harum-scarum tom-boys, probably due to the reaction against a strict Victorian upbringing, as in the case of my Aunt Doris Haig. One of the beautiful Vivian twins, she and her sister Violet were maids of honour to both Queen Victoria and Queen Alexandra. She was a girl who loved practical jokes and horse-play, but this was not appreciated by her considerably older husband, Douglas Haig, Colonel of 17th Lancers. When his regiment was stationed in India and he went off on a tour of inspection into the hills, Doris Haig relieved the monotony of a dull evening by organizing a pig-sticking contest after dinner, in the billiards room. A pawky officer was selected to play the part of the boar. The rest of the officers were horses, and from them the ladies chose their mounts. In the middle of the chase, as they were pursuing the 'boar' round the table, sticking him with billiard-cues, the door was flung open and Colonel Haig stood gazing sternly on the scene. In my Aunt's words, 'He was not at all understanding about our little game.'

Riddles were also in fashion at this time, and they too were of a simple nature, as will be seen from the following:

Q. What is the difference between the Prince of Wales, an orphan, a bald-headed man and a gorilla?

A. The first is the heir apparent, the second has n'er a parent, and the third has no hair apparent, while the fourth has a hairy parent.

Q. What is the difference between your last will and testament and a man who has eaten as much as he can?

A. One is signed and dated and the other is dined and sated.

Q. Why was Ruth very rude to Boaz?

A. Because she pulled his ears and trod on his corn.

The conversation in the great houses where the Edwardians held their mammoth shooting parties could not have been particularly brilliant. It was far more important to be a good shot than a wit. After the day's sport and the heavy eating in the marquees which were run up for a four-course luncheon in the middle of the pheasant slaughter, a hostesses' problem was how to entertain the guests in the long gas-lit evenings. Big houses such as Chatsworth produced elaborate private theatricals with amateur talent provided by guests such as Lady Maud Warrender and Miss Muriel Wilson, while Princess Daisy of Pless used to give musical monologues – the stage set for either an elaborate drawing-room or a desert island.

The over-stuffed and over-spoiled Edwardian gentlemen, after the port, were not always the liveliest company. But besides cards, there was another pastime, ever popular, which did not tax the brains with small talk, for in the same way that 'in the spring a young man's fancy lightly turns to thoughts of love', in the autumn the enterprising old cocks of the nineties were ready for other birds than the feathered kind, and a good hostess would see there was no shortage of these. Husbands and wives arrived and departed together decorously, but they usually had some extra-marital liaison and their paramours would be among the invited. No married couple would be given a single bedroom to share, there would always be a dressing-room, not necessarily next door. Nobody paid any attention to the creaks and groans which issued from the old boards in the night, as slippered feet crept down the passages on amatory excursions. Any nocturnal disturbance was put down to the ghosts.

But sometimes there were scandals in the course of these visits and tongues wagged afterwards. During one of them, a lovely, full-blooded young wife, married to an octogenarian peer, made the most of the occasion by receiving a nocturnal visitor to her room. He was a mere sexagenarian, but such an adventure proved too much for the old rip who had indulged freely in a heavy dinner of many courses followed by a plethora of port, and he collapsed in her bed with a heart attack.

A young blood staying in the house was woken by the sound of muffled thuds and a scraping noise. He lit a candle and tightened the cord of his frogged brocade dressing-gown before going out to investigate. On the stairs he saw his host's young wife. At first he thought her hands were raised in prayer, and then he realized that on her back was an inert male body – the body of one of his fellow guests which she was holding by the wrists as she lugged him down the stairs.

'Help me, good friend, to dispose of this creature that goes bump in the night,' she pleaded.

The dressing-gowned Galahad relieved the lady of her embarassing burden, bedded the overcome sexagenarian respectably in his own room, kept her secret and married the young woman when her octogenarian husband died some years later.

And so the game went on, but always the conventions were supposed to be respected. As Mrs Patrick Campbell had boomed in her deep contralto voice, 'It doesn't matter what you do in the bedroom as long as you don't do it in the street and frighten the horses.'

Divorce was considered common; it was letting down the side. Any sexual abnormality meant exile abroad, or worse. 'He was *such* a charming young man, none of us had the slightest idea, of *course* he had to commit suicide, and now poor Cordelia can't find anyone to be her swan at the ball.'

All the latest gossip was repeated and discussed in the servants' hall, and the goings-on of the nobs were eagerly followed by Rosa who set her sights according to theirs. The cockney Rosa of Leyton, now in the full flowering of her beauty, was firmly grafted on to the lush and vulgar Edwardian tree.

Chapter Three

Winston Churchill was a schoolboy when Rosa first went to work for his mother. During the holidays he was always popping in and out of the kitchen, pestering the pretty young cook with questions and helping himself to succulent tid-bits. Sometimes she would lose patience with him and chase him out of the door, waving a ladle as she shouted, 'Hop it, copper-nob!'

The kitchen at 50 Grosvenor Square (Lord and Lady Randolph moved house in 1892) was a hive of activity, for the merry-go-round of entertaining rarely ceased. Lady Randolph would confer with Rosa over the menus and together they recalled the guests' gastronomic preferences and fads.

'We'll have to cross out the lobster patties, my lady, with Mrs Hwfa-Williams coming to lunch. Shellfish always brings her out in spots.'

'Rosa, His Highness is dining tonight. We'll give him those plain boiled truffles he enjoys so much. They looked enchanting, as you served them last time, like little ebony apples, in that silver dish, wrapped around with a white linen napkin.'

The Prince's taste in food and wine was well known, but it needed the combined intuition and experiments of a hostess such as Lady Randolph and a cook like Rosa to discover something out of the ordinary which would titillate the royal taste-buds. No doubt His Highness suffered from a plethora of rich food for he was not nicknamed 'Prince Tum-Tum' for nothing and even his yearly cure at some Continental spa does not seem to have been very rigorous. At Homburg, for instance, hi régime was an early breakfast of tea, rusks, boiled or fried eggs; meat or fish, green vegetables and a compôte of fruit for lunch; and a dinner, described as 'simple', then bed at ten o'clock.†

Although Rosa had such affection for Lady Randolph, she did not remain with her in a permanent capacity for long, although she always made herself available to cook for her heroine on any important occasion. She never had any difficulty in finding employment and when it became known that the Prince preferred her cooking to any other, she was in greater demand than ever. Her presence in the kitchen was the best bait with which to hook a royal fish.

There was much rivalry in smart Edwardian circles over the Prince and Princess of Wales's frequent Saturday to Monday, and Friday to Tuesday, visits to country-houses. Many epicurean dainties were purchased from abroad to be hoarded in cupboards and stillrooms 'to make a dainty dish to set before a King'. There was no knowing when H.R.H. might turn up, for when visiting in the country he was likely to make an afternoon drive and drop in on some neighbouring house unannounced, particularly if there was one close by which had a reputation for good living. It was a case of 'Prepare thyself for thou knowest not when thy Prince cometh', and so the best grocers were ransacked to lay in stores of his favourite biscuits and bottles of Carlsbad plums, while brandy cherries and boxes of preserved fruit from Nice were held virgin in order to be sacrificed royally.

Whenever the Prince and Princess of Wales honoured a house ptarmigan pie would certainly feature on the menu. The ptarmigan was a game bird beloved by the Edwardians. It

† Edward Legge, *King Edward in his true colours*.

always had a place on the sideboard amongst the cold collation, which provided reserve forces to emphasize a hearty breakfast.

When Rosa was engaged to do the cooking at a country house where the Prince of Wales was being entertained, she made backstairs inquiries as to which of her dishes he appeared to relish the most. She learned from His Highness's valet that he grumbled about sloppy sauces which spilt down his shirt-front, and made a mental note to avoid these. Realizing that variety and surprise were essential to a palate which from over-indulgence had become jaded, she made the experiment of putting a generous dash of sherry in the *consommé* – a daring move, since the Victorians had considered it vulgar to lace the cooking with wine and their precepts still held. But Rosa believed that this practice warmed the stomach, putting it in a mellow mood for the reception of the meal to come and acting as an *amuse gueule*. The Prince approved, and it became the fashion.

In all Rosa's travelling about, working in the smartest houses, both in London and the country, she never lacked admirers either above or below stairs; but her heart remained untouched. There was nothing prudish in her nature, and in bawdy company she could swear with the best of them and listen unshocked to a salacious story. She was 'one of the boys in the backroom' and, since there was much that was masculine in her nature, men felt at ease in her company. But of course there were kisses and cuddles, slap and tickle, smacks on the bottom, propositions rejected and sometimes accepted. And no doubt the kisses were easier to return after a glass or two of champagne.

Rosa had now reached the age of 25. Her parents, on the rare occasions when she went home, always asked when she was going to find a husband. They hoped she would marry Excelsior Lewis, a friend of the family four years older than Rosa, who was butler to Sir Andrew Clarke. He and his sister Laura were the illegitimate children of Miss Mary Cubitt Siely Chiney Lewis of Horsham St Faith, Norwich. Rosa's parents knew that he had money of his own, having saved enough to make a substantial nest-egg. His ambition was to invest this in a lodging house which he and Rosa would run together. The Ovendens approved of the plan and added their persuasion to Excelsior's. This combined effort eventually overcame Rosa's independent spirit.

Years later I asked her if she had been in love with her husband. 'It wasn't the real thing,' she said. 'You see, he was a bit of a dud, but other people loved him.'

When questioned by Mary Lawton on this subject, Rosa was reported as saying, 'My family threatened to shoot me if I didn't marry him, so I did.' But as she never paid much heed to what her family said and had flown so far from the nest, this seems unconvincing. Furthermore the Ovendens were not the kind of people to indulge in anything so dramatic as shooting, neither is there any reason to think that this was a case of 'a shot-gun wedding'.

Although Rosa said her family drove her into this marriage, they were not present on June 13th, 1893, when she married Excelsior Lewis at Trinity Church, St Marylebone. The witnesses were her sister Marianne and Edwin Hills. Rosa wore her every-day clothes, and simply took the afternoon off. No celebration was held, and there was not an immediate honeymoon.

It was a marriage by special licence, which means that the banns were not called in church. According to the existing records, Excelsior gave the address of his employers' house, while Rosa simply wrote 'Parish of Holy Trinity, Brompton'.

She seems to have had some reason for wishing to conceal the wedding, since, apart from the somewhat vague address she gave, she also entered her father's name as Edwin Ovenden instead of William Ovenden. (Edwin was his second name.)

At this time she was working for Charles Duff, a popular member of the Prince of Wales's set who had a house in the Parish of Trinity. Michael Harrison has suggested that it might have been considered compromising had she given a bachelor's house as her address. This is no doubt the reason why she omitted it, for she always believed in discretion and throughout her life enjoyed complicating an issue because she thought it would throw people off the scent.

Excelsior had originally tried to persuade her to marry him in a registry office, but here she had a glib excuse – such a form of marriage would be against her religious principles. Then one day he had turned up with the *fait accompli* of a special licence in his pocket, and in a moment of weakness, rather than let him waste his money, she agreed to go through with it. This, at least, is what she is reputed to have told Mary Lawton. She is also reported as having said that she threw the ring in her husband's face immediately after the ceremony and left him at the church door.

I find this account hard to believe. It is more likely that Rosa was either concealing something or trying to make a good story of it. Otherwise why her deceptively naïve excuse for her alleged violence: 'You see I hadn't lived with him yet so I didn't feel I was married to him.'

My own opinion is that she really cherished some tender feelings for Excelsior but he turned out a great disappointment to her. There was no doubt that he adored her, and Rosa later admitted that she remained faithful to him throughout the years of their marriage.

After a belated honeymoon – probably the only time they were happy together – they made an attempt to settle down into a conventional middle-class married life. With their combined savings they had taken over the lease of 55 Eaton Terrace from Miss Thynne, a relative of the Marquess of Bath. This they opened as a select and expensive lodging-house for carefully vetted clients. The house divided easily in two. Rosa and Excelsior lived in the bottom half while the top rooms were let.

There was very little to occupy Rosa's burning energy since five servants were employed in the house, including a woman to help in the kitchen. The lodgers were only provided with breakfast, and it seemed pointless cooking for Excelsior who, after a session in the Duke of Wellington – the pub a few doors away – could hardly tell the difference between one of her quail puddings and toad in the hole. Rosa therefore abdicated from the kitchen and her copper pots and pans lost their bright burnish.

Boredom, for the first and perhaps the only time in her life, descended upon her like a London fog, tarnishing her gaiety, dimming the bright lights and cutting her off from all the fun of the fair. Poor gloomy Excelsior, like a link-boy, tried to lead her through the darkness, carrying the torch of his affection to guide her. But Rosa was capricious and bad-tempered. It irritated her when her husband was demonstrative. No wonder the poor fellow was 'a bit of a dud' where love-making was concerned, for she mocked him as she avoided his kisses and broke away from his embraces.

> *'Wayward as the swallow overhead at set of sun*
> *She whom I love is hard to catch and conquer,*
> *Hard, but O the glory of the winning were she won!'†*

† George Meredith, *Love in the Valley.*

But Excelsior never won Rosa. A weak character, he tried to drown his matrimonial grief at the pub. Worse still, he made the fatal mistake of asking his sister Laura to come and live with them. Rosa had always detested her sister-in-law and as soon as she moved into the house the fur began to fly.

To escape from the tedium of home life, Excelsior's protestations of love and his sister's hated presence, Rosa bought herself a bicycle and used to pedal off on sad and solitary excursions. (Did she, I wonder, wear the fashionable garment designed by Mrs Bloomer for this new activity? And which of the latest make of machine did she ride, 'The Little Queen' or 'The Steel Fairy'?) On her return she would be faced with an inquisition from her husband and sister-in-law.

'You've been away a very long time on that bike of yours,' Laura would remark with a sniff of disapproval. 'Where did you go?' Rosa would answer with a defiant toss of her head, 'To Marlborough House, of course. *You* should go there some day. They say a cat can look at a King, don't they?'

At last, unable to bear this narrow little life any longer, Rosa told her husband that she was going to take up her career again. They needed more money, she explained, and she could bring back three and four times more than the lodging-house produced. Meanwhile Laura would stay on at Eaton Terrace to look after him. Excelsior objected as strongly as he could. He was frantic with jealousy at the idea of his wife returning to cook in some of the bachelor establishments where he knew she would be only too welcome. But Rosa was determined to escape.

When, therefore, she heard that an American family for whom she had previously worked had taken a château in France and were eager to re-engage her, she immediately accepted the post. With the channel between herself and Excelsior, her spirits began to revive.

Chapter Four

On her return from France she found no improvement in the Eaton Terrace household. Her sister-in-law still had that disapproving sniff of hers, and her husband was drinking more heavily than ever.

'The trouble with you is having nothing to do all day,' she told him. 'Why don't you get yourself a job instead of sitting around moping and swilling beer?'

As usual Laura flew to her brother's support: 'If Excelsior hadn't given up a good job to marry you, he would have got to the top of the tree by now. It's you that has pulled him down and made him drink.'

It was fortunate perhaps for all three of them that Rosa never remained in the house for any great length of time since there were now more and more people from outside who wanted her to come and cook for their luncheons and dinner-parties. In fact she soon had so many engagements that it became necessary for her to enlist additional kitchen staff; and as she always preferred to be surrounded by beauty, she chose her kitchen-girls for their appearance as well as their efficiency.

These young collaborators of hers must have looked like a *corps de ballet*, dressed, as she herself was, in spotless white, wearing chefs' hats and high-laced boots, an item essential to Rosa's comfort since she had large feet which needed support when she stood for a long time: an expensive item, too, being made of fine black kid by a fashionable shoemaker and lasting no more than a month before being replaced with yet another pair.

On one occasion, after the 1914 war, when Sir Osbert Sitwell invited her on the spur of the moment to a dinner-party he was giving, Rosa had to refuse. 'I can't go to the Savoy in my cooking boots,' she explained. One has heard of 'Puss in Boots' but never of 'Cook in Boots', though the latter seems a much more sensible idea considering how much cooks suffer from their poor martyred feet.

Rosa's catering operations were planned and executed with the precision of a military manœuvre. Her primary rule, which she never broke, was to do her own marketing. No matter whether she was cooking for the Prince of Wales or for some *parvenu* aspiring to break into the Marlborough House clique, she would invariably be at Covent Garden at five o'clock in the morning so as to have the first pick of the freshest and rarest vegetables.

The kitchen at 55 Eaton Terrace was not a very big one, but Rosa and her team worked there on the day before any big dinner-party, preparing some of the dishes in advance, baking home-made bread, making the salt-sticks (fancied by the Prince of Wales) and the wafer-thin water-biscuits which accompanied the port. Then, on the afternoon of the day the party was to be given, the whole contingent under Rosa's command would move into the client's house, bringing with them the dishes they had already prepared, and take over the kitchen in order to attend to the final details.

Besides doing the marketing herself, Rosa also liked to shop personally at tip-top grocers. She was extremely extravagant, so much so that her clients invariably noted it, despite the general extravagance of the age, but although her bills were often reluctantly accepted, they were always paid in order to retain her services. Never, for instance, would Rosa have consented to cook for Mrs Arthur James, a hostess renowned for her parsimony, who suffered acutely when a second chicken which had been cooked 'just in case' was required at her luncheon-parties. While the dish was being served, she would watch closely to see if the one bird alone was sufficient, and if it was she would hastily scribble 'D.C.S.C.' on the pad in front of her and hand it to the butler. These initials stood for the message: 'Don't Carve Second Chicken.'

The peak of Rosa's catering career was reached in Coronation Year, 1902, when in a single week she provided twenty-nine suppers at balls. Her health and vitality seem to have been indestructible, for there was only time for her to snatch a brief hour's sleep at the end of each ball, before hurrying off to the market and starting preparations for the following evening. When people said, 'Rosa Lewis is going to do the supper', it was an accurate forecast of a good party.

It was about this time that Rosa discovered a grocer called Jackson in Piccadilly, a small and select shop which carried a remarkably good stock, including various home-made jams, preserves and bottled fruit. As a side-line, Rosa began selling them the Virginian peach-cured hams that she herself prepared. This talent had been acquired while working for Mr William Low of Charleston, Carolina, a sporting crony of the Prince of Wales and owner of a big house in Warwickshire. It was dashing Willie Low who aroused Excelsior's jealousy more than any of the other swells, for Rosa was always dropping his name, speaking of him with exaggerated admiration, as she recalled the lavishness of his entertaining, the delicacies of his table and cellar, his ability to bring down brace after brace of pheasants with his quick left and right as well as charm any other bird off a tree with his *risqué* jokes and high spirits.

In his kitchen at Wellsbourne Park Rosa made friends with his old coloured cook, Mosianna, and Joe, the negro butler, both of whom had been slaves to his father-in-law, General Gordon, before the Civil War. Mosianna initiated her into the secrets of making perfect rice and gave her many recipes for Southern cooking. She learnt how to make waffles which were served with hot maple syrup from Vermont – an innovation to London Society – and after Willie Low had made her a present of a waffle iron, she was often enlisted to preside over a Waffle Stall at the charity bazaars organized by her clients. For these she dressed in her usual impeccable white, with her chef's cap set very straight on top of her coils of bright brown hair, shod in her invariable cooking-boots, and supported by her band of kitchen beauties. The waffles sold like hot cakes.

Since the peach-cured hams continued to do good business, Jackson's now gave Rosa orders for chutney and preserves as well. Soon these too became so popular that the demand for them far exceeded the supply. Not unnaturally Rosa's business association with the manager of the shop developed in time into a firm friendship.

While chatting with her one day he told her that round the corner, at 81 Jermyn Street, the lease of a small hotel called the Cavendish was for sale. The place had been previously known as Miller's and had changed hands many times but had always kept its clientele. As long ago as 1848 it had been successfully managed by a woman called, by a strange coincidence, Mrs Rose, when it had many permanent residents in addition to other clients who used it as a London headquarters. Its present owner, Santiago Franco, now wished to retire. The lease still had nine more years to run, and could then be renewed.

Rosa listened to all this information eagerly. Her forget-me-not blue eyes blazed with excitement when she heard that the little hotel had a big, light kitchen and was patronized by the wealthy and well-born. She began to make calculations. The remainder of the lease would cost her £600 a year. That wasn't much. She could easily afford it, with the amount she was making these days. It would be as easy as pie to persuade Excelsior to sell the lodging-house and invest the money in the hotel. Besides, here at last was a perfect job for him. He could run the place with the help of Laura and this would give him something to do and might keep him away from the bottle.

The idea of the hotel providing an occupation for her husband was the deciding factor. She would buy the remainder of the lease in Excelsior's name and engage a first-class staff. The rest was up to him. She herself would not even live in the building. All she wanted was the use of that big, light kitchen in which to carry on her catering activities.

When this plan was unfolded to Excelsior, he put up no objection, welcoming any sail on his bleak and empty horizon. And so, in 1902, the Cavendish Hotel once more changed hands.

But Excelsior once again proved a disappointment. As an hotelier he was unmethodical, extravagant and lazy. In his cups he would describe his matrimonial troubles to any pretty woman who cared to listen, and there were some who were delighted to offer him consolation. Worse still, he began to splash money around just like one of the swells Rosa was always cramming down his throat. He gave up drinking beer, took to expensive wines, dined off the finest Dover soles and kept hansom cabs waiting outside the front door for hours.

Inevitably the hotel began to go downhill. Clients started leaving, never to return, and even the servants handed in their notice; but having given her husband a free hand to run the place, Rosa still refrained from interfering. It was only when her friend at Jacksons told her that the local tradespeople were threatening to stop her husband's credit, since he never paid his bills, that she was forced to take action. She asked Excelsior to produce the accounts. To her dismay she found that none had been kept. Faced now with the undeniable fact that her husband was a millstone round her neck, she decided to let him go bankrupt and do nothing more to help him. If she was to survive in the precarious seas she had charted for herself, she must cut herself free from him, although she knew that without her he would certainly sink. She therefore hardened her heart against him for ever.

Her first move was to obtain possession of the cash-box, which she cunningly hid in the oven. With this safely concealed, she gave vent to her feelings. Brandishing a carving knife, she drove Excelsior and the hated Laura out into the street, hastening their exit with a volley of pots and pans, of cups and saucers, which whistled over the fugitives' heads and crashed about their heels. So terrified were they of the wild maenad into which Rosa was transformed that they never again set foot inside the Cavendish.

Left to herself in the hotel, with hardly any servants, Rosa sent for her lawyer and arranged to instigate divorce proceedings. It was only too easy to obtain whatever evidence was necessary since Excelsior had been in the habit of making sozzled rounds of the town, trying to pick up crumbs of sympathy and love. Once free from him, she wiped him off the slate of her memory, preferring never to speak or think of him again, for he was the only person in her life of whom she was ashamed: her only failure.

In order to protect the tradespeople to whom Excelsior owed

money, and to save the good name of the hotel, she promised to pay all the debts in full. They amounted to £5,000. She settled the most pressing ones immediately but, after paying the expenses of the divorce as well, had no money left for the remainder. To earn this she worked as she had never worked before.

First of all she pared down the hotel staff to a minimum, doing all the cooking herself. Every morning she was up before dawn, pushing a hand-barrow to Covent Garden Market, loading it up with her purchases and pushing it back to the Cavendish. She had always had a shrewd and expert eye in the choice of a quail, and she now applied this selective gift, buying birds in the market at fourpence and then making a round to private customers and shops to sell them at three shillings each. Meanwhile she spent not a penny on her clothes and only ate once a day. There was hardly any time for her even to sleep at night.

None of her patrons or clients had an inkling of her troubles and she was far too proud to ask for financial help. Somehow she managed to fulfil all her catering commitments in addition to running the hotel, and who could object if she made whatever she could on the side? Who should blame her, for instance, if she always returned, after cooking for a shoot, in a hansom cab bulging with game which she sold at a profit.

Sixteen months after she had thrown Excelsior out, she had made enough to pay all his creditors in full. She had saved the good name of the Cavendish and could now concentrate on its development.

Chapter Five

While cooking in other people's houses, Rosa had always kept her eyes open, carefully observing the furniture and the pictures, the flower arrangements and the lighting, the silver and the china, and the table and bed linen. As a result she had already begun to develop the taste that she manifested later in her life. She wanted her hotel to be different from any other, to be imbued above all with the atmosphere of a big country house in which nothing was too new – a house gay and fresh with old-fashioned glazed chintzes and panelled walls painted white or dove-grey. Instead of opulent Turkey carpets, she would have polished floors and Aubusson rugs. To the fashionable ormolu furniture and spindly gold chairs she preferred winged arm-chairs and broad comfortable sofas. Nor did she want a lot of plush and gilt, but a mellow lived-in setting.

The people who came to stay at the Cavendish would find peace and quiet, for in the days before the vulgar blare of motor-horns, the evenings in Jermyn Street were disturbed only by the clip-clop of hansom cabs as the Quality passed on their way to dine in St James's Square, then one of the most fashionable areas. Rosa's hotel was well situated, only a few minutes' drive from Buckingham Palace, close to clubs such as White's, Boodle's and Brooks's; within walking distance of the Park, Bond Street and the best shops.

Since she did not wish to open her doors to every Tom, Dick and Harry, she decided to divide the rooms into suites, each with its own bathroom. (She liked the kind of baths she had seen in country houses, surrounded with mahogany panels.) Each suite would have its own private dining-room, and there would be no public one. One of these suites she set aside for the use of King Edward, who, as Prince of Wales, had already patronized the hotel under Franco's management. Here he would be able to give dinner-parties and entertain his favourite ladies just as if he was in a friend's house, and Rosa would be there to cook for him and to see to all his requirements personally. The King naturally paid her for these rooms but did not, as has been suggested, give her any other financial assistance.

In those days there were very few respectable restaurants in which to dine out. Lord and Lady Randolph Churchill, when they first married, could only find the St James's Hotel (now the Berkeley), where, according to her memoirs, there was a dingy dining-room lighted with gas and 'an apology of a dinner'. Later the Bachelor's Club and the New Club at Covent Garden became fashionable resorts for dinner. As to hotels, Claridges and the Ritz did not then exist, only the Carlton and the Grosvenor were well established, though Brown's also had some support from the gentry. But the choice was limited. When, therefore, the Cavendish was launched under Rosa's broad-minded management, with its private dining-rooms and superlative cooking, it must have provided a veritable haven, particularly for those who wished to dine out discreetly – provided, of course, they had a sufficiently well-lined purse to meet the bills.

One of Rosa's first guests was Lord Ribblesdale, known to the Prince of Wales's cronies as 'The Ancestor', since in his patrician looks lay the very essence of nobility. Many of the Edwardians were singularly undistinguished in physical appearance, and beside them Lord Ribblesdale must have stood out like a potential Derby winner in a field of cart-horses.

As a boy he had lived for several years in France, where his parents went to recoup from one of many financial crises caused by his father's gambling habits. After leaving Harrow, he again spent some time in France before joining the 60th Rifles. Shortly afterwards his father committed suicide. By then he had married Charlotte Tennant, a girl endowed with shining beauty, intelligence, sweetness and, fortunately, a certain amount of money. Her sister Margot was later to become Margot Asquith. This marriage was an idyll. Lord Ribblesdale had simple tastes and delighted most of all in what he called a *pot au feu* life with his family at his country house, Gisburne, riding through the green valley of the Ribble, larking over fences, followed by Charty, his bright golden-headed wife, their two sons and his eldest daughter, in a joyous cavalcade of beauty. At night he liked to sit cosily in front of the fire, wearing his bedroom slippers, browsing over his favourite classics which he read both in French and English. He was a talented draughtsman, and certainly one of the finest horsemen of his generation.

In 1880, he was appointed as a Lord in Waiting to Queen Victoria, and the book he subsequently wrote, *Impressions and Memories*, gives some intimate pictures of the Queen and Court life at Buckingham Palace and at Windsor:

'I liked my room looking out over the North terrace to Slough and Ditton, a wide panorama peopled by the fine elms which adorn the Thames Valley, indigo-green at midsummer, golden in October, and purplish in March. One resided in one's bedroom – at least I did – and seldom visited the formal and bare equerries' sitting-room. I had a capital roomy writing-table, lots of well-chosen stationery, an armchair and a sofa of merit. The supply of coal was unstinted, and a scarlet-liveried footman brought me an excellent tea in the afternoon. The room itself was on the same floor as the library.'

Another passage shows how well he understood the Queen's temperament:

'I had by this time picked up a sort of working philosophy of the Queen – I knew when she was amused; amused and pleased. I knew this by one of the rare smiles, as different as possible to the civil variety which, overtired, uninterested, or thinking about something else, she contributed to the conversation of her visitors.'

In February 1887, he took his seat in the House of Lords, which was to become a primary interest in his life. He later became chief Liberal Whip, and was an excellent speaker both in Parliament or at the dinner-table. His wit was subtle, gentle, and elegant. Perhaps his wife thought that he was incapable of attacking an adversary unkindly, for on one occasion, before he was going to make a speech, she sent him a telegram saying, 'Hit hard and always below the belt.'

In 1892, he received a second royal appointment, as Master of the Buckhounds. In those days the holder of this appointment headed the royal procession up the course for the opening of Ascot races, and Lord Ribblesdale must have cut a handsome figure in the uniform dating from the reign of Queen Anne – a dark green coat with a broad gold embroidered belt from which dangled gold hound couples – as he rode a showy chestnut called Curious, 'conspicuous for action and colour as its rider was for looks and horsemanship'.†

† Barbara Wilson, *Dear Youth.*

It was during this time that Rosa first met him. Recommended by the Prince of Wales, she went to cook for him at Englemere Green where he had a hunting box and entertained during Ascot week.

His family was already a large one: two sons, Thomas and Charles; and three daughters, Barbara, Laura and Diana, the last two known as 'the dolls'. They were all educated by 'Zellie', their adored and adoring German governess, who came to them as a young girl and stayed with them all her life, eventually taking on the education of the next generation. Her story was later written by the eldest of her charges.†

The elder son, Thomas, joined the 10th Hussars and when he left with his regiment for the Boer War he was so missed by his parents that they both followed him out to South Africa, where The Ancestor, wearing an old covert coat and armed only with an umbrella, rode with the Flying Column. In 1902, when the war was over, father and son spent the whole winter hunting together with the Quorn, Cottesmore and Belvoir, but once again Thomas was called overseas to rejoin his regiment in India. Unable to reconcile himself to peacetime soldiering in the Raj, he applied to be sent on special service to Somaliland where he was made chief remount officer. After the Battle of Jidbali, in which he won the D.S.O., he volunteered to carry dispatches and, while engaged on this dangerous mission, was killed.

This united and happy family were cruelly ill-fated, and The Ancestor, for all his good looks, charm and culture, was haunted by a destiny which, in depriving him of his loved ones, brought him under a dark cloud of melancholy. Charty, his adored wife, whom he called his Angel Queen, developed tuberculosis and for several years had to lead the life of an invalid. She died in 1911, in the same year as his mother, to

† Barbara Wilson, *Dear Youth*.

whom he was devoted. This double loss, combined with his son's earlier death, plunged him into the deepest grief and he seemed inconsolable in his despair.

In her inimitable way Rosa managed to revive this moribund man whom she admired as the most perfect of all gentlemen. She insisted that he left Green Street and put her best suite in the Cavendish at his disposal. When he moved in there she protected him like a tigress, seeing that no one intruded upon him unnecessarily. When he desired company she brought his friends to see him.

At the Cavendish there were many advantages for a lonely man like him, including the atmosphere of a club combined with the privacy of his own rooms. Eventually he sold his house and brought all his furniture to the hotel, giving Rosa what was left after he had furnished his suite. Some of the best pieces she owned originally belonged to him, including the exquisite Chinese Chippendale mirrors.

People may have wagged their tongues when Lord Ribblesdale moved into Mrs Lewis's hotel, and no doubt this removal gave rise to a myth, which persisted until quite recently, that not only did he give her the hotel in the first place but was also her lover. Certainly there was a very close bond of friendship between them, but there is no evidence that this ever developed into a love affair.

The Ancestor had that blessed gift of being able to mix with ordinary people, making them feel perfectly natural and at ease with him, for he never lost the common touch. When he was Master of the Buckhounds he would often drop in at his huntsman's cottage and sit down at the kitchen table for a chat over a cup of tea. In the same way, while living at the Cavendish he sometimes accompanied Rosa out shopping or for a stroll in St James's Park. They must have been a remarkably handsome pair, and as they walked down St James's Street heads of course turned inquisitively in their direction. Once when he had taken her to a theatre someone asked her what the play had been like. 'The kind you would take your cook to,' she answered with a wink.

In his loneliness, Lord Ribblesdale was cheered by Rosa's cockney wit and high spirits. Where other people failed, she could raise a smile. Sometimes he had dark moods when his temper flashed like a steel sword, and she would parry it with the broad blade of her humour. When they had arguments, as they sometimes did over her bills, it was all quickly settled by cutting the cards or by means of a jocular note, such as the following which I found in one of Rosa's scrap-books:

'Madam,

We are instructed by our client Lord Ribblesdale to draw your attention to a communication addressed by him to you last week. May we suggest that this matter indeed demands your immediate attention.

Last, Chance, Ultimatum & Co.'

Gradually he began to take interest in the world again. He was particularly sensitive to female beauty and at the sight of Sir Herbert Beerbohm Tree's daughters, Viola and Iris, who often came to the Cavendish, his spirits revived at once. He already knew and had admired Viola when she played Ariel in Beerbohm Tree's production of *The Tempest* (she must have been strangely tall for this part) and was delighted to meet her again.

In 1912 and 1913, when the two sisters were at their father's house in Rottingdean, they frequently took Lord Ribblesdale for picnics in the Kentish woods and vales, during which fey

Viola would dance barefoot, taller than any hop-pole, and Iris, a blonde Trilby, with her baby-fine hair square cut in a fringe, sat sketching The Ancestor (there was a charming drawing by her at the Cavendish, in which he is wearing large owlish spectacles and a yellow waistcoat) while he chatted away in that distinctive manner of speech of his, rolling his 'r's' and betraying the barest suggestion of a lisp. Iris still recalls how he used to produce pencils and paper and say; 'Shall we play *ve* drrrawing game?' She also recalls a present of his, a coat and skirt of a tweed which seemed to have a magical quality, for it never wore out.

It was a surprise to many and a shock to some when Lord Ribblesdale eventually married Ava Willing, the widow of John Jacob Astor, for although she had beauty and riches she was a hard and worldly woman, with none of the intellectual gifts and lightness of touch of his golden first wife, Charty. Disapproving of this match Rosa inevitably made suggestive puns on her maiden name and was probably not sorry to see her leave the Cavendish, where the honeymoon was spent, even though she was desolate at the departure of her hero who now moved into his new wife's house.

As age crept upon him, Lord Ribblesdale must have felt a great loneliness without his loved ones: his daughters dispersed, no more horses to ride or wild oats to sow. London seemed desolate . . . embers and ashes. The dark depression returned and never left him until he died.

Before Lord Ribblesdale left the Cavendish, he gave Rosa a copy of the famous portrait which Sargent painted of him and which he presented to the Tate Gallery where it now hangs as a memorial to his two sons.

In after years Rosa would look at this portrait and raise her glass of champagne as she said, 'Here's to Lordy – the greatest gentleman of them all.'

Chapter Six

Another of Rosa's early patrons was Sir William Eden. Like Lord Ribblesdale, in his latter years he was unhappy and lonely, and when he came to live at the Cavendish Rosa spread her wings to protect and shelter him, surrounded him with comfort, jealously guarded his privacy and provided his dining-rooms with the best food in London. He and Lord Ribblesdale had much else in common. Both were superb horsemen, men of taste, wide readers, and talented water-colourists. Lord Ribblesdale did caricatures for his own amusement, and line and wash drawings of sporting scenes, while Sir William was touched with real genius. After one of his exhibitions George Moore wrote: 'Sir William is an amateur. We use the word in its original sense and can conceive therefore no higher epithet of commendation. There are too few amateurs among us . . . A glance at the picture shows that he is a painter who travels rather than a traveller who paints. . . .'

Again like Lord Ribblesdale, Sir William made friends easily with ordinary people. Although he could be intimidating, his servants were deeply devoted to him and he would unburden himself to his valet, Woolger, who remained with him until he died. But, for all his intelligence and wit, he must have been impossible to live with. Doing everything so excellently himself, he was hypercritical of others. His standards were set excessively high, and, expecting so much of people, he was constantly disappointed and disillusioned.

His love of beauty made him resent, to the point of violence, anything that he found unharmonious. The colour red was forbidden in his garden and the sight of scarlet geraniums and salvias made him lay about flower-pots with his walking-stick. An errand boy whistling below his windows would fill him with thoughts of assassination. He detested the sight of the Albert Memorial, and loathed the new front of Buckingham Palace, Bond Street, Pont Street and Mount Street, while Harrods was anathema to him. But he loved St James's Street with its dignified Georgian buildings: Boodle's, Brooks's, Arthur's and White's. So he moved, in 1911, from his town house in Old Queen Street to 18 Duke Street, which was next-door to the Cavendish and was then being run as an annex by Mrs Lewis. Eventually he made an arrangement with her to have a wall knocked down, which afforded him a private entrance into the hotel. Preferring things to people, who sometimes exacerbated him so intolerably that he would cut himself off from them altogether, he would often retreat for days on end to these new apartments of his, where he painted, read and wrote peppery letters to the newspapers.

He was closest to the happiness which he never attained when living at Windlestone, his country house in Durham. A perfectionist in the running of his estate, he enjoyed working with his foresters in the woods and took infinite pleasure in the lay-out of his garden, mingling misty blues and deep purple, mauve and silvery-greys, and never a touch of the hated red.

No horseman ever rode more brilliantly to hounds, and for many years he was Master of the South Durham. A quick and graceful shot, he is remembered shooting thirty-eight high pheasants in quick succession out of a possible forty. Once, when asked by one of his guns if hen pheasants were to be shot he answered: 'Shoot everything. Shoot the Holy Ghost if He comes out.' That evening, as the butler handed round an ornate blancmange at dinner, he shouted down the table at his wife: 'Christ! What a pudding!' (No doubt it was made of strawberries or some other red fruit.)

Curiously enough – for he was a professed atheist – his blasphemies, both oral and written, were often interspersed with quotations from the Bible to enforce an argument or make a point.

He kept his body trained to a lean and wiry state of athletic perfection and rejoiced in boxing, at which he seemed to be able to work off some of his pent-up internal combustion, sparring with Bat Mullens and with Bombardier Wells. Sometimes he refereed gory pugilistic encounters between his estate workers, and once, in 1912, staged a fight in the dining-room of the Cavendish before an audience of waiters and a few chosen friends. Rosa was advised in advance of this impending event by a letter which she subsequently treasured in her scrap book:

'Windlestone.

'Dear Mrs Lewis,

I am coming up crowned in glory on Tuesday. The Hon. Ashley too. Now look you 'ere. I shall have a dinner-party that night – noblemen, gentlemen, women, ladies, and prize-fighters – and we will box in the dining-room after.

See?

Tell your Lord Ribblesdale I want him, dinner and after, and anyone else you may think of – pretty – either sex – none but the brave deserve the fair.

W. E.'

This contest, in which Bombardier Wells punched Sid Smith on the nose and 'tapped the claret', as the gentlemen of the fancy used to say, caused just the right amount of scandal to give Rosa a laugh and enhance her reputation with the more dashing elements of Society. It also set the seal on Lord Ribblesdale and Sir William's friendship, as another letter in Rosa's scrap-book shows:

'Dear Lord Ribblesdale,

Lunch with me Cavendish 1.15 on 8th and on to my private view – there is no need to praise or buy – and will you bring that pretty girl, I forget her name, *avec les jolies dents* and right amount of false colour. I will try Pamela, and Lady Scarbrough is coming, at least so she says. I am laid up again with gout that damnable virtue which will have its reward.

Ever,

William Eden.'

Sometimes Lady Eden would also stay at the Cavendish, and Sir William's children on their way through London would occasionally drop in to see their father brooding like a cross old bear in his Duke Street den. Rosa would then have a newly-baked cake waiting for young Anthony* or an overflowing hamper for his elder brother Timothy† to take back to school with him. (These items were eventually entered on their father's account, without his having been consulted, which would lead to yet another passage of arms between him and Rosa.) But it was their sister, Marjorie,‡ who appealed most to Rosa, and a portrait by Swan used to hang in the Cavendish (it now hangs in Lord Avon's house in Wiltshire) showing this lovely dark-eyed little girl standing on a stool, wearing a long stiff dress, like a Velazquez infanta.

* Now Lord Avon.

† The late Sir Timothy Eden.

‡ Later the Countess of Warwick.

The friendship between Rosa and Sir William remained unshaken to the last. She never allowed herself to be browbeaten by the alarming old baronet, but always stood up to him, enjoying it all the more when he flew into a tantrum. She laughed when he raged and the insulting notes of complaint which he wrote were carefully preserved. Here is one example of them:

'Mrs Lewis – Charming Woman!
    Will you *please* turn out that damned dog before I have to murder it or *you* – you for choice!
                        Yours in ever increasing affection,
                                        Sir William.'

And by way of contrast, another:

                        'Windlestone, Dec. 8th, 1912.
                *Circumstances alter cases
                Broken noses alter faces.*
    'I am coming up on Tuesday, and her ladyship too. She had better have the usual room with the maid in the closet hard by – no one will touch her.'

And yet another:

'Woman – have you washed the blankets and swept the crumbs since I left? – Must have a good dinner. I have had O but filth since I left. I want fried fillets of sole, roast neck of beautiful sheep. Quails *à la* Mrs Lewis *et voilà tout*. W. E.'

On one occasion he wrote complaining that Rosa had not addressed a letter to him correctly, so she replied with another beginning, 'Dear Sir William, *Bart*,' apologizing for her ignorance and signing herself 'Rose Lewis, *Bart*.' One of the last, written the year before he died, betrays an even greater irritation than usual:

'May 25th, 1914.
Dear Madam,

I am sorry to complain and needs must when the devil drives, and you are the devil whilst you are amusing yourself which is all you do with your lovers, your dogs, your cocktails and your caterwauling.'

Sir William's quarrels were many, and in his crabbish and perverse way he cherished a really good enemy. His most famous dispute, which led to a celebrated legal fight, was with Whistler.

Sir William admired Whistler more than any contemporary painter and felt that he alone could do justice to the beauty of Lady Eden and produce the sort of portrait of her that in his mind was evoked by the lines:

> *'If one could have that little head of hers*
> *Painted on a background of pure gold.'*

He therefore asked George Moore to act as an intermediary and sound out Whistler as to the price of such a portrait. Moore wrote back a little vaguely, saying he thought it would cost Sir William a hundred and fifty pounds. To this sum Sir William agreed.

After many sittings Whistler painted a tiny portrait, about twelve inches high, of Lady Eden reclining in the corner of a sofa, wearing a golden-bronze dress, against a brown background. This was exhibited in Paris, and catalogued under the title 'Brown and Gold. A Portrait of Lady E.'

Sir William, who was usually a very generous man, felt he had been over-charged since the picture was so minute. When it came to paying, he handed Whistler a cheque on Valentine's Day, saying 'Here's your Valentine' – a harmless little joke, but one which infuriated Whistler, and all the more when he found the cheque was made out for only a hundred guineas. Nor was he appeased by Sir William's covering letter expressing admiration for the picture: 'It will always be of inestimable value to me, and will be handed down as an heirloom as long as heirlooms last.' But he refrained from showing his anger and simply replied:

'Dear Sir William,

I have your Valentine. You really are magnificent and have scored all round.

I can only hope that the little picture will prove slightly worthy of all of us, and I rely on Lady Eden's promise to let me add the few last touches we know of. She has been so courageous and kind all along in doing her part. With best wishes for your journey.

Very faithfully,
J. McNeill Whistler.'

Lady Eden, however, received no reply from her letters asking for an appointment for the final sitting, and when Sir William demanded the immediate return of the picture there was still complete silence from Whistler. Realizing he would never recover the portrait in any other way, Sir William then started legal proceedings against the painter in Paris.

The day before the case was due to be heard, on March 5th 1895, Whistler informed the prosecutor that he had painted out Lady Eden's 'little head', replacing it with that of a model.

The case went against him – Sir William, to everyone's surprise, proving a remarkably good witness, remaining cool, calm and clear when cross-examined – he was ordered to deliver the portrait, replace the head of Lady Eden, and pay a thousand francs damages. He promptly lodged an appeal and meanwhile wrote many letters to the Press, and a spiteful facetious little book entitled *The Butterfly and the Baronet*, which he read aloud whenever he could.

In 1897 his appeal was heard and the final judgement delivered. He was to keep the picture on condition that he made it unrecognizable as a portrait of Lady Eden, he was to return the hundred guineas with 5 per cent interest, and he was to pay a thousand francs damages with interest and the cost of the first trial, while Sir William was to pay the cost of the appeal.

The baronet represented all that Whistler had hated in England and this dislike for him now became so intense that he quarrelled with any of his acquaintances who spoke to him. Sickert was a friend of both, and wished to take neither side. Whistler, hearing Sickert had been seen in Sir William's company, returned his card when he came to call, with 'Judas Iscariot' scrawled across it.

Since he and Sir William were extremely belligerent, it is a wonder that this quarrel never came to the fisticuffs which both indulged in, for Whistler also took lessons from a professional pugilist. Rossetti summed him up accurately when he wrote these lines:

> 'There's a combative artist called Whistler
> Who is, like his own hog's hairs, a bristler.
> A tube of white lead
> Or a punch on the head
> Offer varied attractions to Whistler.'

Whistler once challenged George Moore to a duel, but the only answer he received was a scathing critical review of his painting by Moore in a newspaper. Whistler was very free with his taunts and used to say, 'I always like calling a man but I always have the sense to know that he is unlikely to come.' But the truculent baron would certainly have accepted his challenge.

Although Sir William had so many quarrels and lost most of his men friends, women always forgave him. The path of their friendship with him must have been hazardous. He complained furiously over unpunctuality and objected to smoking and scent; he did not like the presence of children, and abhorred dogs. None of his women friends who wished to remain in his good graces would have risked wearing so much as a red ribbon trimming a dress; but in spite of all his idiosyncrasies, none of them could forget the force of his character. Lady Cunard used to say that he was the cleverest man in London; his family sometimes declared he was the most selfish man in England. Perhaps they were both right.

He died at the Cavendish in 1915 during the first year of the War, in which three of his sons were killed. The eldest, Timothy, who succeeded him to the title, wrote *Trials and Tribulations of a Baronet*, and in the pages of this most remarkable and moving book the angry old aristocrat, with all his intolerance and brilliance, will live for ever.

Chapter Seven

In following the course of Rosa's two most favoured guests – 'the cook's young men', as they were affectionately called – we have sailed ahead in the history of the hotel. We must now go back to the beginning of the century when she had taken over the management of the Cavendish at the age of 35.

From photographs of her taken at this time one sees she had a remarkably trim waist which was accentuated by a belt fastened with an engraved buckle. She wore her masses of brown hair in the style of those elegant ladies in Helleu portraits combed upwards off her forehead, puffed out into a halo and coiled on top of her head. Her fine white lawn blouses were high-necked and made with rows of tiny tucks running down the front; the white serge skirts she favoured were moulded to her splendid figure and cut with a slight fullness at the back, giving the suggestion of a train. Her stately carriage and dignified appearance had earned her the nickname of 'The Duchess of Jermyn Street'. It was sometimes disconcerting when the Duchess opened her mouth and emitted a torrent of expletives.

Rosa had developed a keen eye for property, and made shrewd negotiations with her landlords, the Maudsley Trust† when she obtained from them the additional lease of the land which faced Mason's Yard. She had already acquired the use of the houses on either side of the hotel, and in 1904 she had been

† Apart from the Cavendish, this trust also owned an officially recognized mental institution – no doubt an appropriate coincidence.

able to build a fourth wing, making a quadrangle enclosing the gardens at the back of the original house which stood at the corner of Jermyn Street and Duke Street, St James's. This not only added to the size of the property but meant that the Cavendish could boast of a row of well-appointed suites, whose occupants could enjoy the privacy of the hotel's courtyard and garden. And should some unwelcome guest come in unexpectedly by one entrance, there were four other doors by which they could make a discreet exit.

Now that the Cavendish had become a much bigger establishment, a public dining-room was needed, and Rosa was able to provide one which looked out on the courtyard garden: a long dove-coloured panelled room flanked with mirrors. This soon became fashionable and at dusk Jermyn Street would echo with the slam of the aprons of hansom cabs, releasing, in front of the Cavendish, wasp-waisted beauties, their pearly shoulders misted in tulle, diamond stars and moons of Diana shining in their hair, accompanied by tail-coated dandies carrying opera-hats under their arms.

That the meals served by Rosa were remarkable can be seen by the following menu, an ordinary everyday one.

Cavendish Hotel
Diner du 26 Juin, 1908
Consommé aux Ailerons
Truite froide à la Cavendish
Blanchailles
Soufflé de Cailles à la Valencienne
Piece de Boeuf à la gelee en Bellevue
Jambon de Prague aux féves
Poularde froide à la Parisienne
Salade

Asperges en branches
Pêches à la Marron
Bombe glacée Dame Blanche
Friandaises
Laitances à la diable.

Meanwhile the King continued to patronize the hotel and Rosa would always hold herself in readiness to cook for him personally. He sometimes enjoyed eating simply, as though he really was plain Mr Jackson or Mr White (two of the aliases he used on the Continent) and at Marlborough House had been known to give little tripe-and-onion suppers, served by a purveyor from the Tottenham Court Road. When supping incognito at the Cavendish his favourite dish was broad beans and bacon with parsley sauce – truly rustic fare reminiscent of the would-be rustic régime indulged in at the Petit Hameau.

The royal presence inevitably added to the hotel's reputation and assured its success. But success in one field alone was not enough for Rosa. Her bubbling spring of energy needed harnessing to further endeavour, and once again she took on outside commitments.

One of the first was to manage the catering of White's Club – an unheard of task for a woman, and which she undertook only for a bet – but she soon resigned when a member complained that she had called him 'a damned old woodcock in tights'. Besides, he had objected to her dog in the dining-room. In 1907, however, on Edward VII's recommendation, she was engaged to cook for the Kaiser at Highcliffe Castle – a job which was far more to her liking, even though the German emperor abhorred anything French, stipulating that he would not have a French chef or cook, and Rosa was a confirmed francophile.

It is strange that the Kaiser should have taken Highcliffe Castle, near Christchurch, for it looked like a French château, being built somewhat in the style of Azay le Rideau with a fine view across the English Channel. Only a moderately large country house, it was scarcely big enough to accommodate the Kaiser's retinue of ninety people.

Feeding this contingent, however, soon presented a problem. Unprepared for the demands made on them, the little village shops ran out of stores and Rosa then had to go to London every day – travelling in state by special train – to do her marketing at Covent Garden and get her groceries at Jackson's. Not only did the Kaiser have the use of private railway facilities during his visit, he was also authorized to use his own postage stamps, specially designed for the occasion (a rare item for philatelists).

She found the Kaiser exceptionally easy to work for, in spite of his whims. Owing to his withered arm he had to use special cutlery, with a knife and fork joined together like Siamese twins, and therefore did not like being served anything that was difficult to cut up or had a lot of small bones. She seems to have ignored his francophobia and drafted all her menus in French, as can be seen by the following, written in her full round handwriting:

Highcliffe Castle
Diner du 7 Novembre
Soupe aux choux
Gigot de chevreuil
Poularde flanquée de Cailles
Pointes d'asperges
Soufflé aux Pruneaux
Gateaux.

Nor did she believe in spoiling the artistic *tout ensemble* of the dinners she prepared by pandering to the imperial prejudices. Classical French dishes were frequently served, and the Kaiser ate them with evident relish. He would not, however, allow French wines to appear at his table, though an exception was made for champagne, and the usual beverages were his own native produce, hocks and dark brown Bavarian beer.

On one of her rare days off, Rosa was invited for a spree on the imperial yacht, the *Hohenzollern*, which did not much impress her as a boat – she thought more of the *Giralda II*† which belonged to Harry McCalmont (my grandmother's second husband) and was at that time the biggest steam yacht afloat. But the super-efficiency of the service aboard the *Hohenzollern* evidently met with her admiration, as did the music played by the German band, for both menu and programme of music have a place in one of her scrapbooks.

Princess Daisy of Pless, Mrs Cornwallis West (formerly Lady Randolph Churchill), the Duchess of Westminster and many other leading hostesses entertained the Kaiser during this visit of his to England and with his permission enlisted Rosa's service for these dinners, as they always had when entertaining Edward VII. Rosa thus found herself cooking for another crowned head in their houses. Her own memento of the imperial visit was a tip of £100, a decoration, a brooch and a signed reproduction of the Kaiser's portrait by Laszlo, all of which he gave to her before sailing back to Germany.

It was at the beginning of the century that Rosa became a friend of Escoffier's. Here indeed was a royal alliance, for she considered

† Later purchased by Alfonso XIII; sunk by the revolutionaries to prevent his escape from Spain.

him to be the King of Chefs, while he paid her the compliment of referring to her as a Queen among Cooks. On a table in Rosa's parlour his photograph, dedicated 'A ma très Chère Amie', stood in a silver frame. It revealed a man of considerable distinction, not unlike a statesman in appearance, with dark penetrating eyes which bespoke a capacity to command, and an imposing Prussian moustache.

Escoffier's career was in many ways similar to Rosa's. Like her, he had started at the bottom of the ladder, working as a boy in his uncle's kitchen at Nice. He too had cooked in great houses, for he went to Russia and became chef to one of the Grand Dukes. During the Franco-Prussian War he served as *chef de cuisine* to the General Staff of the Armies of the Rhine and was captured by the enemy. Subsequently he was chef at the Grand Hotel in Rome, and, at the height of his fame, when he became a friend of Rosa's, was chef at the Carlton. A true artist, he believed that anything beautiful to the taste, in order to achieve true perfection, should also be beautiful to the eye. It is not surprising that a man of such artistic perception should have married a French poetess named Delphine Daffis, who was honoured with an award from the Académie Française.

Rosa always said that Escoffier had taught her more about cooking than anyone else.

In 1908, Rosa was made responsible for the gastronomic meals at Hever Castle given by William Waldorf Astor. This famous American millionaire often stayed at her hotel, where she used to prepare surprises for him in the form of Southern dishes which she had learned to make when she was with Willie Low. He was a discerning gourmet and took immense trouble with his menus, compiling them himself. That they were highly elaborate can be seen from the following:

Hever Castle
Diner du 10 Juillet, 1909
Melon Glacée
Consommé Princesse
Bisque de' Écrevisses
Blanchailles
Suprême de Volaille à la Maréchale
Selle d'Agneau à la Chivry
Foie Gras à la Gelée
Salade Nantaise
Cailles rotis sur canapés
Pêches Rose de Mai
Caroline Glacées
Croutes de Merluche.

Pêches Rose de Mai: what a pretty dish this must have been, so evocative of Rosa herself and one of which Escoffier would have approved. *Cailles sur canapés*: quails featured on most of her big menus and she was faithful to these delicious plump little birds which, it will be remembered, helped to save the fortunes of the dishonoured Cavendish when she bought them cheap in the market and sold them at a profit from her barrow. Indeed, her most famous recipe of all was for quail pudding: 'Take your quail and truss for braising, and leave in marinade for a few hours. Make an ordinary suet paste, line a basin with it, then place your quail, one for each person, in slices of beef as thin as paper, which when cooked dissolve into the sauce; add some fine chopped mushrooms, parsley, shallots and good stock, and put a paste top and boil for one hour. Serve rice or barley with it.'

*   *

One can imagine the feelings of the resident kitchen staff when Rosa and her girls appeared on the scene to prepare for one of these great dinner-parties; understandably the intruders were met with hostility. At first Rosa had done her best to collaborate with the servants of the house, but after various attempts at sabotage on their part, she made a rule to work only with her own employees. The old-established cooks had their noses thoroughly put out of joint by her young assistants, for, having been trained by her, they could get a wage of £100 a year – a great deal of money in those days and far more than was usually paid.

The jealous servants grumbled in the background, complaining of her bad language, commenting on her extravagance, criticizing the amount of cream she used: 'Seems as if she takes a bath in it. . . .' Anything missing or broken was always blamed on Mrs Lewis and her girls. Sometimes Rosa would take over the dining-room, supplying her own waiters, the flowers and gold chairs. At the last moment she would come upstairs for an inspection and, like a high priestess, ceremoniously burn some of Floris's essence called 'Tantivy', to make quite sure that the dining-room was perfumed to her liking.

When she arrived at a country house where she had been engaged to cook for some special occasion, she was always beautifully dressed and must have appeared far more aristocratic than some of the guests, such as dumpy Mrs Ronald Greville, who easily might have been taken for a cook. It was not surprising, therefore, that as Rosa sailed in through the front door, she was often mistaken for a member of the house-party. In this connexion, my grandmother, Mrs Harry McCalmont, used to tell the story of a shooting party at Chieveley Park, where the Prince of Wales, later Edward VII, was one of the guns and Rosa had come to cook. (This story, incidentally, gives yet another version of Rosa's original encounter with H.R.H.)

A cold collation was laid out on the sideboard, and the Prince, feeling peckish, slipped into the dining-room for a pre-prandial snack. There he saw a handsome young woman dressed in white, drinking a glass of champagne. He exchanged a few pleasant words and, before hurrying back to the drawing-room, gave her a kiss. A few minutes later, when the luncheon-party had assembled, he turned to my grandmother and said:

'Your most beautiful guest is missing.'

'But all my guests are here, Sir.'

'Not the lovely lady in white whom I saw just now by the sideboard with a glass of champagne in her hand. Now who was she, Winifr-r-red?'

'That must have been Mrs Lewis, the cook.'

'Hmmm . . . I gave her a kiss.'

'We shall certainly have a very excellent dinner, then.'

Although Rosa had no difficulty in capturing gentlemen's hearts, which gentleman managed to capture hers? (No easy task, as poor Excelsior Lewis had learned.) Her love affairs are difficult to trace since she believed they should be carried on discreetly in a *sub-rosa* fashion. She also disapproved of the habit of keeping love-letters. 'No letters, no lawyers and kiss my baby's bottom!' was one of her original aphorisms.

There was only one person in whom she may have confided completely – her friend, Edith Jeffery, who would never betray any of her confidences. I have, however, reason to believe that Rosa was in love with William Low, who in his heyday must have been a most attractive man. Lord Ribblesdale was, in her opinion, the finest gentleman, but rich roystering Willie Low from Charleston, Carolina, was her Southern beau, and he flitted in and out of the Cavendish scene laden with gifts of peach-fed hams, sweet corn, molasses and Southern comfort.

Since he was a first-rate shot and enjoyed fox-hunting, he bought an estate in Warwickshire, where he could indulge in these sports and where he entertained his friends, including the Prince of Wales who often stayed with him and for whom of course Rosa came to cook. At Warwick races, he kept open house in the club-room and Rosa had the difficult task of providing lunches for an unknown number of guests. She was less worried by this problem, however, than by the ardour of her employer, who was a connoisseur not only of four-footed fillies but also of the two-footed variety, and was as adept in the boudoir as in the field of sport. But it was not so much these aptitudes of his that worried her as the presence of his wife in the background.

In his declining years, alas, Willie Low took to the bottle and when he died left all his money to another woman.

There was another candidate for Rosa's heart. He was called Major Leigh, a lean, soldierly looking, dark-haired man with a moustache. I believe he was killed in a motoring accident, and after his death Rosa harboured a resentful suspicion against cars; 'You know where you are with horses but you can't trust those damned machines . . . they're out to get you,' she would warn young men as they roared off in fast cars. Sometimes she would stand on the steps of her hotel and shake her fist at one of the hated vehicles revving up noisily. Rosa inherited Major Leigh's cellar. On very special occasions she would say, 'We'll have one of Major Leigh's bottles,' but otherwise she never mentioned him, for 'she never told her love', and if questioned would shut up like a sea-anemone before a probing touch.

With Rosa, therefore, it was evidently a case of 'I love my love with an L' (Lewis, Low and Leigh) and although the first two were not altogether up to snuff, I believe she was happy with the third.

Like most exceptional women, Rosa was not entirely feminine. Lord Ribblesdale recognized this when he told her that by nature she was a seventh-part man. As a child she had always wanted to be a boy. She was a heroine worshipper and regarded herself as 'one of the lads', preferring a jolly bunch of fellows and the pleasures of the table and cellar to those of the double bed, the divan or tiger-skin.

Her attitude to casual admirers may be judged by the way in which she dealt with a certain Frenchman who prided himself on his amorous conquests. Having invited her out to a tête-à-tête dinner, he arrived rather early at the Cavendish carrying a big bunch of red roses. Rosa invited him into her sitting-room, where she opened a bottle of champagne. Encouraged by this he sat beside her on the sofa and began embracing her passionately. Struggling out of his arms, she stood up in front of him and pulled her skirts up to her knees: 'Take a bloody good look at these,' she said, 'for you're not going to see any of the rest of me tonight, or any other night, so if you don't think it's worth-while taking me out for a meal, you'd better go and find a nice clean tart in Piccadilly.' This so amused the Frenchman that he took her out to a more expensive restaurant than he had at first intended, and remained a life-long friend of hers.

Further evidence of Rosa's attitude to would-be lovers is provided by this anonymous rhyme which I found in one of the scrapbooks:

'When'er I come and when'er I go
I get a smile from Rosa.
Perhaps a kiss or two or so,
At three she answers "No sir!"'

Chapter Eight

In 1909 Rosa achieved one of her greatest triumphs, being asked by the Foreign Office to organize and prepare their banquet. Commenting on this, the *Daily Telegraph* reported:

'Ministerial banquets on the eve of the opening of Parliament or in the celebration of the King's birthday possess an interest for the ordinary mortal distinct from the dinners, however important, that are given on other occasions. The careful housewife is apt to wonder what are the resources of a great government department to choose a well-chosen dinner of the conventional succession of course, and whether new or wonderful dishes often figure in the menu. Of course, in very many instances the Minister who is giving the banquet simply calls in one of the leading firms of caterers, and has no further responsibility in the matter until the bill is sent in. At the Foreign Office, however, the system in recent years has been different and on Monday night, when Lord Crewe gave his full-dress dinner, as in 1908, all the arrangements were undertaken by Mrs Lewis, the well-known cook, who is not only proprietress of the Cavendish Hotel in Jermyn Street, but is called in by the most exclusive houses in London, when the dinner or ball-supper is to be something quite exceptional.'

Three years later she was paid a similar compliment, this time by the Admiralty, when she was invited to cater for their banquet. Here is the menu on that occasion:

Admiralty, le 24 Juillet, 1912
Melon Glacée
Consommé de Volaille
Potage Bisque
Truite Saumonée Norvégienne
Blanchailles
Soufflé de Cailles au riz
Jambon de Prague
Dindonneaux Froids
Salade
Glace d'Ananas
Pêches Bonne Femme

Our greatest woman cooking expert, Elizabeth David, to whom I showed some of Rosa's menus, confirmed my own opinion that they were exceptionally well chosen, better balanced than most of that date and more original.

After these two striking successes Rosa seriously considered retiring from the catering field, for it seemed there were no further heights for her to scale. But she could never resist taking on the arrangements for a smart ball, since she enjoyed the party so much and would usually make a personal appearance in the ballroom, whether invited or not.

It proved a profitable idea when she found an empty house, 27 Grosvenor Square, which she furnished beautifully for dances, charging her clients for its hire. Here Lord Ribblesdale gave the coming-out dance for his lovely daughter, Diana, the youngest of 'the dolls'. It became known as 'Rosa's Grosvenor Square House', so no wonder she used to feel that she was giving the ball herself and had a right to share in the fun.

In the *Gourmet's Guide to London*, by Lieutenant-Colonel Newnham Davies, published in 1914, there is a whole chapter devoted to the Cavendish Hotel. Of Rosa herself the author remarks: 'A menu of one of Mrs Lewis's ball-suppers at Surrey House may well find a place here. She, I believe, first made the great discovery that young men who have danced an evening through prefer eggs and bacon and lager beer, in the small hours of the morning, to *pâté de foie gras* and champagne.

Chaud
Consommé de Volaille
Cailles Schnilten
Poussin à la Richelieu
Poulet Grillé, pommes soufflés.

Froid
Petites Crabes. Homard. Truite au bleu.
Poularde en Gelée
Dindonneaux Hezedia
Canard pressé en Parfait
Boeuf et Agneau à la Mode
Mousse de Jambon en Bellevue
Asperges
Fraises du Bois Monte Carlo
Mélange de Fruits
Pâtisserie
Café Noir

(à *dix heures*)
Grenouilles à la Lyonnaise
Oeufs poches au Lard
Rognons Grillés
Pilsener Lager Beer.'

The author goes on to describe how he 'drew from Mrs Lewis some opinions as to the change in dinners she had noticed since she first began to rule the roast. One difference is a matter of finance, that people in Victorian days were quite content to pay three guineas a head for a dinner, but that now hostesses bargain that their dinners shall not cost them more than a guinea a head. Dinners have become much shorter, but people in Society have a greater knowledge of gastronomy than they used to possess.'

Colonel Newnham Davies was once invited by Rosa to a luncheon party where she broke the rule she laid down that three dishes are the right number at any lunch. The description he gives of the meal makes one's mouth water:

'Our first dish was of grilled oysters and celery root on thin silver skewers, and then came one of those delicious quail puddings which are one of Mrs Lewis's inventions and for which King Edward had a special liking. There was a whole quail under the paste cover for everyone at table, with a wonderful gravy, to the making of which go all sorts of good things and which when it has soaked into the bottom layer of paste makes that not the least delicate part of the dish. This was followed by a dish of chicken wings in breadcrumbs and kidneys, before the pears and pancakes, an admirable combination, with which our lunch ended.'

Although Rosa now abandoned catering in private houses, she would still go and cook for Mrs Patrick Campbell when her splendid appetite happened to be flagging – a rare occurrence and to her a sign of real illness. There was a time when Rosa had thought very poorly of Mrs Pat. This was when she had bolted with Lady Randolph's second husband, George Cornwallis West, which caused a hoo-ha of gossip loud enough to 'frighten the horses in the street', but, as usual, Mrs Pat was forgiven.

*   *

84

Edward VII's appreciation of Rosa's cooking was also shared by his wife, the 'Sea King's daughter from over the sea' whose sweet nature matched her loveliness, and among Rosa's treasures was a letter from one of Queen Alexandra's ladies-in-waiting, Lady Rachel Dudley, in which she said: 'I am sure you will be glad to hear that the Queen was so pleased with your dinner that she sent Miss Knollys the next day to ask me for one of the menus. I also had a letter from Lord Knollys to say the King thought it was an excellent dinner.'

But it was not only Rosa's cooking that the King appreciated. He was also genuinely amused by her and, after some of the mealy-mouthed sycophants in his usual entourage, she must have seemed like a salty sea-breeze blowing through a stuffy conservatory. Before the Prince and Princess of Wales succeeded to the throne there were no bounds to what people were prepared to do in order to get into the Marlborough House set. One rich *parvenu* used to gallop closely behind the heels of the Prince's horse when he went out riding in Rotten Row, in the hope that he might be taken for one of His Royal Highness's friends. One day his horse bolted and crashed into the Prince's, causing it to fall. This gave rise to a song called 'The Galloping Snob of Rotten Row'.

In reference to courtiers and the King's friends about this time, *Modern Society* commented:

'Manners at Sandringham are a fine art which only the born courtier can master. The visits not being of state, the strict rules of etiquette are relaxed; but respect for royalty must not be forgotten. The person who can converse with Royalty without relapsing into familiarity will succeed where others fail. This is the true secret of the surprising success of some of the *nouveaux riches* as compared with the total failure of others much richer. The first are born courtiers and very good company. The second are either shy or blatant vulgarians.'

Rosa must have been 'a born courtier', knowing just when to make a *risqué* remark and shock a party into life with an injection of spicy language. Her timing was as good in dealing with people as it was in preparing a complicated dish, and it was this, combined with her discretion and culinary genius, which appealed to her royal patrons.

Prince Tum-Tum had an eye as well as a stomach for cooks. In 1904, when staying with Sir John Fisher at Admiralty House, Portsmouth, he was so attracted by the youth and beauty of his host's cook, Mrs Baker, that he invited her to stay at Buckingham Palace to see how a great State dinner was arranged. It is just as well that Rosa was not there at the same time, for the combination of both these presences in the royal kitchen would certainly have borne out the proverb about too many cooks spoiling the broth!

The King's death in 1910 was a great sorrow for the nation, but a greater sorrow still for Rosa. It was subsequently said that she benefited financially from the King's will. This is untrue. But the contents of his private cellar remained at the Cavendish and his grandson must have enjoyed the usufruct of this same fifteen years later, when, as Prince of Wales, he also patronized the hotel.

Nor did Rosa receive any valuable jewellery from Edward VII, who was never particularly lavish with his presents. When he went to India, for instance, he brought back an immense amount of gifts from the bazaars, ranging from gold vases for a lady friend to a cheap walking-stick which he presented to the cricketer Buller, after chastizing him with it as a joke. His usual gifts were little boxes, and some of his cronies had enough of these to stock an emporium. Their value varied according to the respective recipients' degree of friendship: some received Battersea enamel boxes, others were given ones of Benares brass or carved ivory; occasionally a favourite might be honoured with one designed by Fabergé and set with jewels.

When I first went to the Cavendish I was told, 'You must see Rosa Lewis's corsets signed by Edward VII.' These had great notoriety and she kept them as a sort of autograph book. I did see them, and have retained a vivid picture in my memory of signatures scrawled all over the whale-bones with which they were reinforced, making a pattern like cuneiform. There were names of actors and actresses, writers, painters, musicians, sculptors, jockeys, boxers, millionaires, Society beauties and débutantes. Yet although I have racked my brains I cannot remember if I actually saw the signature of King Edward VII among them.

During the fashionable craze for treasure hunts which swept London in the early thirties, these famous corsets of Rosa's inevitably figured on the list of objects which had to be secured. Nobody ever managed to capture them, however, since Rosa always waylaid the hunters as they arrived and produced so much champagne that the chase fizzled out.

On one occasion a sailor friend of mine pranced out into Jermyn Street after a party wearing the by now notorious garment over his underpants. But in later years it disappeared from view: I imagine Edith did not approve of the exhibit and when it was mentioned she would change the subject with an adroitness which she had learned from Rosa.

*   *

It was in 1908 that the American polo team began to make the Cavendish their London headquarters. When they were staying there the atmosphere was that of a hilarious house-party. Rosa adored these good-looking, rich and lively young men – Devereux Milburn, Watson Webb (a brilliant left-handed player), C. C. Rumsey, L. E. Stoddard and especially Tommy Hitchcock – and invited pretty girls to meet them: girls she could trust not to get her young American gentlemen into trouble and who would give them a good time and keep the corks popping.

It was about then that she started using the 'Elinor Glyn' for special parties. Apart from the name this room had no association with the red-headed novelist, who was not a habituée of the hotel, but Rosa called it after her, believing it to have the seductive atmosphere of her best-seller *Three Weeks*. It was one of the prettiest rooms I have ever known: beautifully proportioned, with white panelled walls and a very fine Adam chimney-piece. Rosa had furnished it with Sheraton and Hepplewhite furniture. In a corner was the biggest sofa I have ever set eyes on – four people could have slept on it comfortably – covered with a glazed mauve chintz and piled high with lavender, apple-green and rose-pink cushions. A Chippendale cabinet against one wall contained Rosa's collection of Toby-jugs. Here the American team used to celebrate their victories.

Rosa now began to take a lively interest in polo, watching her darlings play at Hurlingham and Ranelagh, cheering them on with uncontrolled enthusiasm. To her it was not an international game, but the Home Team playing for the Cavendish against the Outsiders. She must have been a regal-looking supporter, wearing a sweeping pearl-grey coat and skirt, a touch of lace at throat and wrists, and a leghorn straw hat trimmed with a black velvet ribbon and a rose.

There were many photographs of th...
in her gallery of loved ones, and the ...
the winning goal in 1909 was on...
sessions.

Having reached the age of 44, she could now...
and enjoy herself in her hotel and make further in...
In 1911 she enlarged the kitchen so that it ran the full le...
the three houses. It was cheerful, light and well ventilated, wi...
windows opening out on a courtyard at the back. At the same
time she also added on to the laundry.

As time went by she came to regard the Cavendish almost as
her ancestral home – a home where children were particularly
spoilt and which met with the full approval of visiting valets
and maids who were provided with their own sitting-rooms.
'You treat my house like an hotel!' Rosa once expostulated
when a guest had displeased her. Some of her friends certainly
treated it as a stronghold impregnable to newspaper men in
search of an interview, bailiffs in pursuit of a victim, and angry
wives armed with notional rolling-pins. On the big table in
the hall piles of letters waited to be collected by those who used
the place as a convenient address. The visitors' book did not
belie its name. One signed it at the end of a visit, and not, like an
hotel register, at the beginning. And it was never made available for divorce evidence.

From America, in 1912, could be heard the faint beat of a new
and stirring rhythm, which finally hit our shores in a burst of
syncopation with 'Alexander's Ragtime Band'. Soon everyone
in London was whistling and humming this tune. Ethel Levy's
'Itchy Koo' and 'Everybody's Doing It' followed. Then the
'Bunny Hug' came over and was soon all the rage.

syncopated days intimate supper parties were given
...ate suites of the Cavendish. Stage-door Johnnies,
...and knuts would entertain fashionable actresses there
...the theatre, and sprigs of nobility would treat their
...urite Gaiety Girl to one of Mrs Lewis's suppers. Rosa
...ways knew which rooms would be most suitable for the requirements of the evening, made sure that the lights were softly
shaded, and arranged cut-glass vases of roses, and sweet-peas,
sprigged with London-pride, in such a way as not to obstruct
the view of a pretty face across the supper table.

Although the tunes and the fashions were changing, she herself remained faithful to her Busvine coats and skirts. Her
evening dresses were few but expensive, designed by Jay's and
Worth, long enough to sweep the ground, and made of black
or white satin or of velvet. She invariably wore the swinging
string of amber, which she called 'my yaller beads', and her
scent, 'Red Rose', came from Floris's, the shop just down the
road. By this time her beautiful brown hair was beginning to
turn grey.

The years before the 1914 War were profitable ones for the
Cavendish. The clientele consisted not only of the rich and
famous, but also of a curious coven of dowagers, who stayed
there regularly, and a smattering of clergymen some of whom
were distinctly eccentric. There was one whose opening conversational gambit was: 'Curious thing . . . none of my family
ever grows his canine teeth.'

Rosa was very fond of her gentlemen of the cloth and, in her
inimitable way, could tailor her conversation to suit the drunken
scallywags and then, at the sight of a pair of gaiters approach-
ing, abruptly forswear the obscenities and become the kindly
God-fearing woman that any bishop would respect.

Through the years she had evolved a certain philosophy,

which she now put into practice. There were some people, she thought, who had all the money in the world and didn't know how to spend it properly, while there were others with nothing but an overdraft at the bank: young men with titles too, sons of fathers she had known . . . it didn't seem fair. So, in Robin Hood fashion, she charged the poor no more than a nominal sum and added the rest of their bills to those of the rich.

She also made sure that no party was given at the Cavendish without her being the principal guest, thus deriving the dual benefit of being paid for the champagne that was provided and being its chief consumer. 'If you can't have your cake and eat it,' she would say, 'you can have your champagne and drink it.'

Chapter Nine

By the end of the 1914 War, which brought Rosa greater sorrow than she had ever known, her hair had turned white. Although she had never wished for children of her own, she had a suppressed maternal instinct which she was able to release in the affection she showered upon the sons of her friends, many of whom she had known since birth. 'I knew him before he was born,' she would say affectionately, and to these boys the Cavendish had been like a second home.

The terrible casualty lists tore at her heart, announcing every day the loss of all the gilded youth she had known so well. The cruel Nemesis which dogged Lord Ribblesdale's family struck again: among the first to be killed was his son-in-law, Percy Wyndham, who had married his daughter Diana only a few months previously. His younger son, Charles Lister, died of wounds in August 1916, on the hospital ship that was moving him from Alexandria. He had previously been wounded twice.

In the same year Sir William Eden died. How Rosa must have missed the angry old baronet: his tantrums, the high standards he exacted which were a challenge she enjoyed, those teasing, witty notes, the complaints and sly compliments. In his commonplace book his last entry was a Persian quotation: 'The Worm of the World hath eaten out my heart'. The same worm gnawed at Rosa's heart, but the resilience of her nature buoyed up her spirits and to comfort herself a little, she bought a puppy, the first Kippy, a shaggy-haired Aberdeen terrier who was to develop a character as capricious and impudent as his owner's.

On the declaration of war, Rosa had banished the signed portrait of the Kaiser to the gentlemen's cloakroom – 'That's the only throne for old Willy,' she said, as she viciously hammered in a nail with the heel of her shoe to hang the picture above the lavatory seat – and when the war was over she sent him back the order he had given her, but kept his brooch.

Mounting emotion broke in a great wave of jingoism. Clara Butt sang her famous patriotic songs, Mrs Lewis distributed white feathers indiscriminately, sometimes making terrible gaffes, and Kippy, her Aberdeen terrier, was trained to fly at the heels of any man who was not in uniform.

Officers on short leave from France made a bee-line for Rosa and the honeycomb of the Cavendish. Bills were forgotten, but if some rich foreign fish rose in the pool, he was inevitably hooked to pay the piper and keep the merry-go-round turning. For if it stopped for a moment there would be nothing left but tears and heartbreak.

At the beginning of the war, Rosa had been at the very top of the financial tree. Her catering alone was making £6,000 a year. By the time the Armistice was signed, she had lost an enormous amount of money. Many years later she showed Sir Shane Leslie (the nephew of her heroine, Lady Randolph Churchill) a desk with a drawer full of bundles of cheques tied with red, white and blue ribbons. 'My war effort,' she said with a sigh. 'Some of them stumers, I should think . . . I don't know, for I never cashed them to see. Lots of these were written by the ones who never came back. Thousands of pounds here. Anyway . . . they had a good time while it lasted.'

The Irish Guards were her favourite regiment and she always kept rooms for the wives of married officers spending a few days' leave in London. Some of these ladies buckled to and gave her a hand in the hotel when there was a drastic shortage of servants. They must have been very fond of Rosa since they organized a regimental subscription to buy her a magnificent sable coat; she wore this until she died and always referred to it as 'my sables of sin'.

The men who stayed at the Cavendish on leave were treated like the fighting cocks they were; free champagne flowed, and in the Elinor Glyn, the horrors of Passchendaele mud, the gas attacks, the rats in the trenches and the barbed wire were forgotten. Rosa bought a set of musical instruments and the noise of the Cavendish jazz band could be heard out in Jermyn Street above the noise of the air-raids as the cymbals clashed, the trap-drums rattled and voices bawled out the choruses of 'Take me back to dear old Blighty', 'Tipperary', 'Keep the home fires burning' and Mrs Lewis's favourite, 'K-K-K-Katy'.

Rosa made a point of calling every man herself on the morning he was returning to the front, bringing him up breakfast in bed and a farewell gift of a parcel containing cigars, cigarettes, a bottle of wine or champagne, as well as rare delicacies from Jackson's and Fortnum and Mason's, which she was able to wheedle out of her shopkeeping friends without producing the necessary food coupons.

Sometimes she went to Victoria Station in her big Daimler, returning to the Cavendish with a car-load of men who had nowhere to stay for the night. Here they found every delight from a hot bath to 'a nice clean tart', if the obliging Irish countess who usually stayed in the hotel was not available.

Although Rosa's outside catering was now at a standstill because of the war, many farewell parties were given in the

Elinor Glyn room, where Kitchener dined before the fatal voyage in the *Hampshire*, during which he was drowned. Rosa liked this stern, shy man but said that both he and General Roberts were totally lacking in any culinary sense. Food to them was just fodder; you might as well have given them nose-bags – unlike the Quarter-Master General, that most attractive man General Cowans, whom she accepted as an all-round connoisseur both of cooking and beautiful women.

Lloyd George and Asquith also gave dinner-parties in the Elinor Glyn, and Rosa's cooking and fine cellar served to mellow sensibilities exacerbated by the acrimony of political discussion.

Perhaps it was Willie Low who had first planted the seed of love for America in Rosa's heart. This seed had flourished and grown in the sunshine which the polo boys brought with them. She now made a great fuss of all the young Americans who had enlisted under the British colours. Among these was Caroll Carstairs, who joined the Grenadier Guards and was severely wounded. In the novel he subsequently wrote,† he gives a contemporary picture of the hotel, the 'Bentinckt' and its owner, 'Mrs Oliver':

> 'All Americans anxious to get into the war in 1914 frequented Mrs Oliver's at the Bentinckt Hotel. Here drinks were served and charged to everyone. . . .
>
> 'Something of the excitement, the heightened spirits and energy generated by the war seemed to me to be concentrated in the small space created by the four walls of Mrs Oliver's sitting-room. Through the clouds of cigarette smoke I could see myself in battle; a drink too much and I felt a reckless

† Caroll Carstairs, *A Generation Missing*.

courage in the face of an imagined danger. During these lapses a word or a laugh near me, whose immediate significance was not quite understood, seemed like the encouragement and applause of my brother officers. I would leave the Bentinckt with quite a swagger although I was not even in the Army at the time.'

Another American who enlisted in the English forces was Kingman Douglas, the present husband of Adele Astaire, who joined the R.F.C., and with other members of his squadron stayed at Rosa's whenever they were on leave.

When the United States became our Allies, Rosa hoisted the Stars and Stripes, and 'Over There' became the signature tune of the Cavendish jazz band.

She now had the pleasure of welcoming a second generation of Americans, for fathers would say to their sons, 'When you get to London, go and see Rosa at the Cavendish.' It pleased her when these well-mannered young men invited her out to dinner or took her to the theatre, which to her was just 'the play', whatever she might have seen, for she was unable to distinguish between Martin Harvey in *The Bells* or Denis Eadie in *The Man Who Stayed at Home*.

When the maroons went up announcing the Armistice and the crowds in Trafalgar Square shouted 'Who won the War?' and the answering cry came 'We Won the War', Rosa was there with a Union Jack in one hand and the Stars and Stripes in the other.

It was all over. . . .

She surveyed her hotel. Looks like a broken-down cab horse, she thought. I'll have to give the whole place a thorough spring clean and a lick of fresh paint all round. It'll do no good brooding over all that's lost and gone. There's a new lot coming along – boys like Lord Ribblesdale's grandsons, young Martin and Tony Wilson. And this new Prince of Wales likes to get around, they say – a lively young fellow, with an eye for a pretty girl, like his grandfather, God bless him.

Chapter Ten

The Cavendish never recovered from its war wound and for ever after walked with a limp like a much-decorated veteran.

Rosa was now 51. When peace came she decided not to resume her catering but content herself with the world of her hotel and her house at Jevington, which in her memory she may have associated with the dark horse, Major Leigh. Is it possible that he gave it to her? Here there were many photographs of him, some of them taken on horseback. She never lent the house to anyone and it seemed to be very personal to her.

The Homesteads, as it was called, was near Eastbourne: an Edwardian building with a pretty garden, a greenhouse, an orchard, a small farm and a cottage. The latter was used as a sort of out-patients' department for the Cavendish lame dogs, the alcoholics, the love-lorn, the financially pressed and those on the run from their families. Inmates of the Cavendish would often be cajoled into Rosa's Daimler, thinking they were going for a short spin, and find themselves shanghaied to Sussex for the week-end.

She always returned from these visits looking as blooming as the roses she brought back from her garden. On the return journey the car was packed with punnets of strawberries and baskets of peaches, while hampers of plump country chickens and ducks were stacked on the roof. Sometimes Rosa returned with a sucking-pig in her arms. But although she always appeared 'in the pink' after these excursions, some of the 'out-patients' evidently could not stand the pace and seemed to be in a worse state than when they had set out.

I have never known the Cavendish when it was not occupied by some resident nut or lame dog whom Rosa had taken under her wing. In the twenties, for instance, there was Piggy: I can't remember his surname but I think he must have been a war relic. He appeared to be very rich and was certainly generous since he took a positive delight in paying for everything twice over. His life revolved round the Cavendish and his club. The pattern of his day was to arrive in Rosa's parlour at about twelve o'clock and stand everyone drinks. He usually returned to his club for luncheon, coming back to the hotel for a liquid dinner and staying there to take part in any jollification that might emerge, at the end of which a cab was summoned and he was rolled into it, to be decanted back at the club. Sometimes he could not manage this journey and then Rosa would put him to bed and feed him on turtle soup for a few days. When he was recovering she would take me up to see him, and if he put on my cloche hat and ordered a bottle of champagne it was a sure sign that he was on the mend.

There was another figure who always intrigued me: an immensely old and pink man, small and chubby, spick and span, and shining from bald head to button boots. I think he hibernated like a hedgehog in some upper room during the winter. It was a seasonal sign when, with the first warm days, he appeared in an invalid chair which was pushed out into the courtyard garden and placed beneath a big, striped umbrella. Here, benign but silent, he would sit nibbling cucumber sandwiches and sipping tea. He looked like some endearing mechanical toy from the Nain Bleu. I once asked Rosa who he was. 'A dratted nuisance!' was her reply.

*   *

In the post-war days parties were still given at the Cavendish, but they had a different character. Entertaining was no longer so carefully planned and executed. Dinners and small dances would be arranged on the spur of the moment, invitations were issued over the telephone, and guests – almost certainly to Rosa's disapproval – were more raffish and mixed.

The Cavendish, like a coin, had two separate faces, and no one could predict which might turn up. One face showed all the old ladies, the country cousins and characters out of what might have been a twentieth-century version of one of the Barchester novels. The other presented the bums and the bohemians. Rosa floated at ease between them, presiding with a splendid ubiquity over tea and toast in the drawing-room, while organizing quite different games in other parts of the house.

Those who did not know the Cavendish imagined it was altogether *louche*, a den of iniquity, the scene of orgies; but in reality it was often very dull and respectable, and sometimes it even seemed that the old trout predominated. But, as in roulette, after a long run of black, a spin of the wheel would produce the raffish red once more.

One of Rosa's pets who was drawn into all the festivities was a whimsical eccentric called George Kinnaird, whose mother used to pay an annual visit to the Cavendish. He was not only an asset to any bacchanalian enterprise but also an extremely affectionate son – both of which qualities met with Rosa's approval as she believed that every mother should be properly respected (especially when she happened also to be a Scottish peeress). So she issued an edict to the more notorious party-throwers in her circle: 'We can't have Lady Kinnaird worrying about young George having a good time, and we won't have a good time without young George. So you've all got to mind your P's and Q's and not say a word to any of those dratted small-beer newspaper scribblers. We can't have them putting in a lot of lies about the goings-on here for her ladyship to read.' During her daily chats with George's mother, Rose herself never put a foot wrong, sticking to safe subjects such as royalty, family life, servants and of how much things had deteriorated since the war.

On one of her visits Lady Kinnaird gave a luncheon-party in the Elinor Glyn room for the Queen of Roumania. On this occasion, Rosa superintended the cooking of a perfect meal and then joined a champagne gathering of the riff-raff in her sitting-room, after which she made a dignified entrance to pay her respects to the exalted guest.

Rosa had also known George's grandmother, an excessively evangelical lady, a leader of the Y.W.C.A. and a governor of the Lock Hospital for fallen women. 'She gave me fourteen Bibles, I haven't got a bloody one now,' Rosa used to say, then went on to describe how the old lady had summoned her to help with the hanging of the drawing-room curtains in her St James's Square house. 'We knelt down and had a prayer first. It didn't annoy the Almighty, it pleased her ladyship and it didn't do me no harm – although it was a bit awkward, kneeling with a couple of bottles of bubbly under my petticoats for her two sons waiting in the study.'

Rosa's practice of muddling people's names – originally a deliberate effort to protect her clients – had now become a habit, but one could never be certain whether she indulged in it in order to confuse the issue or merely to show off and get a laugh. Caroll Carstairs has described, for instance, how he was addressed alternately as 'Mr Cardboard' and 'Mr Carsteps' (although his correct name always appeared on the bill). In the same way, a young newcomer who had not (almost literally in this case) yet made his name, would be known as 'that young Kippy' until his character became more firmly established.

Kippy, Rosa's Aberdeen terrier, had developed into a Cavendish fixture. He was the subject of many legends and was reputed to have been smuggled into France in a kit-bag, where he had seen life in the trenches and had swallowed the ribbon of a V.C. during a party given by one of Rosa's generals. He gave himself great airs and seemed to think that he owned the hotel and its purlieus, as he sat at the open window of the parlour with his paws on the sill surveying Jermyn Street. Sometimes he went for long solitary walks in the West End.

Like Rosa, he had his favourites and enemies. The only thing that ever frightened him was a morose-looking camel, employed to advertise a certain brand of cigarettes, which used to parade through the West End in the charge of a negro wearing a burnous and a fez. One day, as this alien beast loped down Jermyn Street doing its soft-shoe shuffle, Kippy went for its heels. It retaliated with a well-aimed kick which sent Kippy flying into the gutter and yelping in terror as it turned its scrawny neck and lifted its lip in a supercilious grin, baring long saffron-coloured teeth. After this fearful experience, Kippy never set foot outside without looking up and down the street and sniffing suspiciously.

It was in the twenties that Edith Jeffery first joined the staff of the Cavendish. Her mother had been a cook and was an old friend of Rosa's. She herself had been trained as a dressmaker and therefore began by helping with the sewing and care of the linen in the hotel, but very soon she became a sort of lady-in-waiting to Rosa, to whom she was a perfect foil. A small gentle woman with brown bead-bright eyes, rather like a character out of a Beatrix Potter book (one of those dear scuttling, snuffling small creatures like Mrs Tittlemouse or Mrs Tiggy-Winkle, with all their busy housewifely characteristics), she was the only person who could really manage Rosa, somewhat in the manner of a mouse controlling a lion. The loyal little mouse was always on the *qui vive* to see that the lion did not roar too loudly or fall into a trap.

When Rosa made her visitations into the outside world, Edith was usually in attendance. By nature she was shy and retiring but Rosa brought her out of her shell, sometimes with the most unpredictable consequences. 'Take Edith' was one of Rosa's phrases when refusing an invitation. In this way Edith found herself flying off from Hendon in a frail aeroplane, with an open cockpit, piloted by a young man who was staying at the Cavendish. She looped the loop over the hotel and has never flown since.

Nor will she ever forget the first sale she went to with Rosa, who prodded her into making a blushing opening bid of a hundred pounds for a Lawrence picture which was subsequently knocked down to another bidder for several thousand guineas. She was only a girl then, but still treasures the catalogue of this sale. Through the years she attended many others, making bids for Rosa.

Rosa could be delightfully incoherent when describing some of the adventures she had with Edith. In a throw-away line she would conjure up a fantastically intriguing picture and then project a second slide on the screen of one's imagination without ever explaining the first. Thus I once heard her say, 'That was the time Edith and I went to Ireland on roller-skates.' And I am still wondering how someone's aunt came to sit on an electric eel 'in one of them Bible countries'.

Edith was particularly kind to children. Small ones staying in the hotel often preferred her to Rosa, who, being so much larger than life, filled them with awe. It was only when they grew older that they began to understand her and speak up in her presence. Not all children can answer back like Alice. But with Edith they felt safe. She would have made a wonderful nanny, and, like the best ones, knew when to put her foot down.

After Lord Ribblesdale married Mrs Astor and moved from the Cavendish, the suite he had occupied was taken on by Evan Morgan, the son of Lord Tredegar, whose turreted castle in Wales with its menagerie of wild beasts endowed him with a fantastic Firbankian aura. His mother, who had the strange hobby of making exquisite copies of birds' nests, was said to have also constructed a human-sized model, lined with dried mud, in which she used to sit. His familiar was a malicious macaw, which terrified his friends and once pecked a black pearl ear-ring off an unsuspecting lady and dropped it in the fire. He himself was *Capa y Spada* to the Pope and, when attending the Holy Father, wore a romantic uniform with a plumed hat. He was also immensely rich. Rosa gave him the entrée to the Cavendish through all its secret doors, and he became one of her most privileged guests.

Sir Harry Clifton was another rich man for whose *fin-de-siècle* appearance and complex character the Cavendish made a very suitable background. He looked like a character out of some Gothic novel: immensely tall and gaunt, with raven-black hair and aquiline features set in a handsome tormented face paler than the gardenia he habitually wore. His personality had many facets, including those of playboy, recluse, poet, *bon-viveur* and mystic. Although he did not keep a permanent suite at the hotel, he was so often there that he was almost an 'inmate'. Rosa considered him a real gentleman of the Old School and liked to help him dress for a Court occasion. 'I must go and rub Harry Clifton with ice before he gets into his knee breeches,' she would announce.

She showed a similar solicitude to Alastair Graham, the nephew of her old admirer Willie Low. In those days he was a wild young man, and she took him under her wing and into her heart, demonstrating her affection by following him around with cups of turtle soup, saying, 'It's only this that keeps him together.'

On one occasion, when travelling across France in a train, having spent the previous night at the Cavendish, he opened his suitcase to take out a book. No sooner had he raised the lid than a fearful toy serpent sprang across the carriage. His books had vanished and in their place were two bottles of champagne, a glass and a clean napkin. When he told Rosa about this later, she said, 'I always put snakes among the wine to distract the attention of the Customs officers.'

Rosa and the Bright Young Things were naturally drawn to each other. She had known their grandfathers and grand-mothers, as well as their fathers and mothers, and seemed to have much in common with some of their more eccentric older relations. She was 'a sport', ready to go anywhere, do anything at the drop of a green hat. Like them, she was adventurous, questioning and resentful of authority, and believed, as they did, that all doors should open before her. They always got a warm and vinous welcome when they descended upon her at all hours of the day and night, not only because they en-couraged parties but because their hedonistic approach to life amused her, and although they were feckless about money and bills, there was usually some Archie Schwert† in tow to pay the piper.

Imagine a summer night in 1923 with the bright young things 'weaving a mad jazz pattern ruled by Pantaloon'. 'Let's go round to Rosa's,' a voice suggests and they all pile into taxis which draw up outside the Cavendish. The night porter, Moon, looking like a cross old turtle, reluctantly opens the door, and in they troop: Brian Howard, Hugh Lygon, David and Olivia Plunket-Green: Lord Ribblesdale's grandson, Martin Wilson, Lettice Lygon, the lily-fair daughter of Lord Beauchamp, and Mark Ogilvie Grant, giving his imitation of Clara Butt singing 'Land of Hope and Glory', followed by his cousin Nina Seafield, a red-haired edition of the young Queen Victoria; Henry Weymouth and Daphne Vivian twanging ukeleles, Michael Rosse and his sister Bridget Parsons, pioneers of the Charleston in Mayfair ballrooms; Nancy Mitford and Hamish Erskine; Elizabeth Ponsonby and Robert Byron, John Sutro and Babe McGusty.

They crowd into the front parlour where Rosa is holding court. She is dressed all in white, with her long string of amber beads knocking against her knees as she advances to welcome them, a glass in one hand and the other engaged in anchoring a wayward lace scarf: 'Well, fancy you all coming in. Old Shrimp Whiskers has just climbed into Mossy-possy's bedroom, and she threw the jerry at him.'

Edith pops her head round the door and eyes the crowd suspiciously. She does not approve of people coming in from outside and ordering drinks after licensing hours.

Rosa rambles on: 'We've just seen the young Professor off on the Flying Scotsman. He came here to buy a horse and got so

† A character in *Vile Bodies* by Evelyn Waugh.

tight that we had to take his trousers and shoes off on the train, otherwise he would have jumped out of the carriage window. Come on into the Elinor Glyn. The five loafers and the two fishies are having a party with cherrybums of champagne. They're all asking for you.'

She leads them through the big hall, which looks like a station waiting-room, with piles of shabby luggage, some of which has stood there for years and is covered with cobwebs. Many of her guests have flitted, leaving behind gun-cases and fishing-rods in lieu of payment. By the fireplace stands a kettle-drum which sounded at Waterloo. Portraits of Nelson's admirals stare blankly out of their frames. Outside the Elinor Glyn a table is stacked with jeroboams of champagne. Their labels, criss-crossed with signatures, are tombstones to spent gaiety, *Où sont les champagnes d'antan?*

Rosa flings open the door. 'Here they all are. There's Snivelling Dick . . . Knew him before he was born. Pots of money. They gave him a gold cigarette-case when his trousers fell down in Piccadilly. Young Evan's upstairs having twins. Lady What's-er-name over there looks like a tart but she isn't. Edith and I stopped her brother marrying that gingerbush. Queen Mary thinks the world of her.'

Steffany, the old, old waiter, shuffles forward – a withered homunculus, deaf and almost blind, hunched over the jeroboam of champagne he carries on a silver salver.

Some hours later . . .

A hush has fallen on the Cavendish. The bright young people have drifted back home or on to other more secret assignments in the night. In the Elinor Glyn all is still; the empty bottles float in the ice-buckets.

In one corner a guards officer in full-dress uniform sits bolt upright, fast asleep. A small door in the panelling is slowly pushed open and in wanders Rosa. She sets down a glass and starts collecting cushions off the sofa. The sleeping officer opens one glazed eye. 'What are you doing with those, Rosa?' he asks.

'Taking them up to young Evan's room.'

The guardee quivers with disapproval. The other eye opens and his monocle drops out.

''Pon my soul, Rosa,' he mutters, 'why do you bother with pansies like that?'

'Pansies?' she snaps. 'And who the hell do you think you are? I saw you leching after that Lady Chatterley, like a tom cat on hot bricks. And when it comes to calling young Evan names, I'd just like to ask where I'd be if it wasn't for pansies like him who pay the bills for scrimshanking buggers like you.'

And with a final withering sniff she collects a few more cushions and sails out of the room.

The sleepy officer shakes himself and, propping his elbow on his bearskin, peeps through the curtains with bleary eyes. A pale light has crept into the garden as another day breaks over the Cavendish.

Chapter Eleven

On December 29th, 1926, with Edith in attendance, Rosa set sail for America in the *Berengeria*. It was a happy voyage and with her usual luck she won the ship's pool. Before the boat docked at New York a tug-load of friends came out to greet her, and journalists swarmed aboard to interview her. Any awkward question she cunningly countered with a deliberate red-herring and, when asked if she could tell them anything about Lord Ribblesdale, she merely replied, 'He liked to dress serious.' Her arrival was announced in the Press and she agreed to give interviews during her visit. In America at least she seemed to be able to swallow her contempt for 'those nosey newspapers'.

A large wicker laundry basket was the only piece of luggage over which she was concerned. 'Let's leave the rest to look after itself,' she told Edith. It contained some of her finest champagne, which she had brought to give American friends, and this sailed through the Customs as though it enjoyed diplomatic immunity. 'I suppose they thought it was just cowslip wine we had made ourselves.' Edith later told me, when describing their journey.

They arrived at the Ritz-Carlton and found the suite of rooms, which had been provided for them by friends, so full of flowers that it looked like a florist's shop. Two hundred telegrams were waiting to greet them. In spite of prohibition, camouflaged bottles of brandy, whisky and gin were delivered at their apartment from anonymous donors. The telephone never stopped ringing, for the friends of forty years were all champing at the bit to be the first to entertain 'The Duchess of Jermyn Street'. Favourites like Oliver Filley, Tommy Hitchcock, the polo boys and Americans who had joined the American forces during the war, were all ready to show Rosa and Edith the sights of New York. Servants who had once worked at the Cavendish made pilgrimages to see her again. A former colleague, a butler named Horace, whom Rosa called 'the old bean,' a severe and dignified figure looking rather like a distinguished member of the House of Lords, escorted her on shopping expeditions. One of her friends provided a car and chauffeur, but she usually preferred to walk.

With some difficulty Edith persuaded Rosa to buy a new hat, but getting her to wear it was quite another matter. On several occasions when they were going to a luncheon party Edith coaxed Rosa to try it on. 'Now you really do look nice, darling,' she told her friend, who only turned away from the looking-glass with an expression of distaste. 'Go and get me a handkerchief out of the bedroom,' she would tell Edith, and then, as soon as her back was turned, Rosa whipped off the smart hat, stuffed it behind a sofa cushion and with a sigh of satisfaction, put on her old green velour. The stuffed birds vibrated triumphantly as she sailed from the room.

When interviewed by the Press Rosa was always questioned about Edward VII's favourite dishes, and this topic led on to what food the then Prince of Wales fancied most. Walter Davenport wrote an article in *Colliers* called 'The Cook's Day Out' (a phrase which Rosa used in describing her holiday). In this he gives the following account of a conversation he had with her:

'The present Prince of Wales will eat almost anything you give him whether it is good for him or not but he is given to worrying about taking on a bit of flesh. I took him in hand about it. "Your health comes first," I told him. "What if you are a bit stoutish? Your grandfather was, and a splendid gentleman he was, if you don't mind."' (The truth was that the Prince of Wales ate very little at this time – not from vanity but because he wished to keep his weight down for riding in point-to-points and steeplechases.)

Commenting on appetites in general, she said, 'The greatest eater I have ever seen was Lady B. Law! how that woman could eat. She was as big as a house – a large house, mind you – and it was nothing for her to eat a five-pound fowl stuffed with truffles, not to speak of the soup and a river pike stuffed and smothered in a cream of prawns and a salad. But she did it with an air which lent a beautiful air of delicacy to what might have been a gastronomic shambles.'

If this female Billy Bunter made a habit of indulging in these dainty snacks 'stuffed with truffles and smothered in cream' her liver also must have been well on the way to becoming 'the size of a house'. But Rosa could not have approved of such a menu. In a long interview she gave to the *New York Times* she said that she supported the 'three-course meal of clear soup, followed by fish or roast fowl, and a sweet.' She praised American meat, and in particular the chops; but she objected to the custom of serving 'a sauce and kidney trimmings' with them. 'A grilled chop should stand or fall on the flavour imported by its own juice which makes it succulent, delicious and epicurean.'

Asked by the Press what was her opinion on prohibition, she said she thought it was 'a lot of bosh which only defeated its own purpose'. She gave cooking tips in various papers but ignored the fact that since Mr Volstead's prohibition law, the field of American cooking had become somewhat restricted.

Champagne, she counselled, should always be served in quart glasses and Virginia ham cooked in beer – 'When it leaves the oven christen it in champagne.'

Her American readers must have wondered where the beer and champagne were to come from unless there was any left in Mrs Lewis's trunks.

Rosa's advice on cooking was nicely spiced with her own particular aphorisms. 'What you have given you still have, and what you have saved you have lost . . . When you're unhappy go out and give yourself a present . . . Always give a sausage a little pat when putting it in the pan: that's what America needs too, a little pat. There's too many edges here.'

Walking down Park Avenue she was again worried by the sharp angles of the high buildings and the innumerable windows placed symmetrically one on top of each other. 'Too new, too sharp,' she said. 'Needs a pat here and there. Yes, America needs smoothing down, that's what it is.'

Another great welcome awaited Rosa and Edith in Washington, where they were put up in style at the Carlton. Rosa called on the speaker, Mr Nicholas Longworth, in his office, and the British Luncheon Club sent her an invitation, making her the first woman to be thus honoured.

One of the objects of her journey had been to sell some enormous tapestries which she had acquired as a surety for a loan of several thousand pounds. They were said to be genuine Gobelins and depicted the life of Constantine the Great, the designs being after Peter Paul Rubens.

An art expert friend, Mr Charles Paulding, took charge of them but, alas, they turned out to be fakes. Yet another of Rosa's bad debts.

At the end of three hectic weeks, Rosa and Edith once again

set sail for home – back to the Cavendish, which was like a ship becalmed without its Captain and Lieutenant. The champagne in the laundry basket had been replaced by parting gifts, but the tapestries – 'those dratted Goblins' – were still with them on the return voyage.

Chapter Twelve

The most famous of the Cavendish servants was Steffany. In one of the visitors' books there are two pencil sketches of him drawn on a fragment of tablecloth by Orpen and Munnings during a dinner-party. Steffany was deaf and very nearly blind. He wore a greasy tail-coat, a tea-stained 'dicky' and looked as if he never took his clothes off. He certainly appeared never to go to bed. There were many extraordinary rumours as to his origin. At various times he was credited with being the Emperor Maximilian's bodyguard, a butler to the Rothschilds, and one of Garibaldi's soldiers. The irreverent even said he had been Rosa's first lover, and, for some inscrutable reason, it was thought that he had changed his name to Steffany after the Tichborne trial. No one knows how these rumours originated, for he spoke to no one.

Shane Leslie, in his novel, *The Anglo-Catholic,* gives a graphic description of him:

'His white mottled face bore the expression of a gargoyle and his skull seemed to be fringed with cobweb. His back was bent like Diogenes in a tub. He moved with ponderous dignity for if Ganymede, the cupbearer of the gods, was his spiritual forefather, his grandmother might well have been the Dowager Empress of China.'

Steffany died in the mid-twenties and was succeeded by Moon, an irascible, skinny old man. Perhaps his grumpiness was due to chronic lack of sleep, for, like Steffany, he never seemed to go to bed. In his latter days he became night-porter, and it became an obsession with some of the guests, returning in the early hours of the morning, to try and coax a frosty icicle of a smile out of him. The only way to succeed was to join hands and dance round him singing, 'Shine on Harvest Moon'.

One of Rosa's first hall-porters was a man called Scott, whom she nicknamed 'Dirty Scott' because of his rooted objection to taking a bath. When he first came to the Cavendish there was no lift and he used to carry all the heavy, old-fashioned trunks up to the bedrooms on his shoulder. The most important thing in his life was his fox terrier, Freddy. Scott did not drink, paid little attention to women and apparently had no vices; Rosa was therefore very surprised one evening when she found him lurking in Piccadilly, with Freddy as usual at his heels.

'Well I never, Dirty Scott!' she exclaimed, 'I believe you're hanging about to pick up a tart.'

'Not me,' he replied earnestly. 'It's this spring weather that's upsetting Freddy. I've got an appointment here with a man who's bringing a nice little fox terrier bitch – just the right size for the little fellow.'

Scott hero-worshipped Lord Ribblesdale and, when the puppies were born, gave him the pick of the litter. It was a terrible day when Freddy died and his broken-hearted master had the body stuffed at great expense and presented it to The Ancestor, who stood it on guard outside his room. 'Just goes to show what a real gentleman his Lordship is,' was Rosa's comment.

She and Scott often had terrible rows; he was sacked or gave notice every few months, but nevertheless stayed on for many years. He once said of Rosa, 'You could love her so much that you could hate her,' which summed up the feelings of a great many of her servants. When he was in her bad books, Lord Ribblesdale defended him, as can be seen from the following newspaper report:

'Another old-fashioned hotel has been used as a permanent residence for some years by a peer of the realm who held an important position with Queen Victoria. He takes real interest in the establishment: helps now and again to draw up a menu, protects the old porter when he receives one of his periodical threats of dismissal, and advises the proprietress on many points of detail. He would hardly be able to do this at a modern Palace Hotel.'

A young cook named Anne Ross, who worked at the Cavendish in 1917, found Rosa an eccentric and capricious mistress. In a letter she wrote to me, she recalls her original interview with her:

'First of all Mrs Lewis talked a little bit about cooking. She was sitting near a small desk, then she got up and started staring at my ears. I was very worried because I thought she was looking to see if they were clean. I'm afraid I very bluntly told her I didn't come here for an ear inspection. "Oh! my dear," she said, "I'm not inspecting your ears, I'm just admiring them. They're such pretty ears."'

She goes on to describe how Rosa, before leaving for a week-end at Jevington, would order all the coals to be taken out of the coal-hole which had to be whitewashed by the time she returned.

Rosa gave her cooks little peace, since she was always drifting in and out of the kitchen, believing that nothing could be done by deputy. If there was trouble below stairs she settled it by taking over the controls herself. Once in the twenties, for instance, a rich young client called Bobby Field invited her out to the Opera. Looking her most magnificent, dressed in black velvet, wearing her loveliest jewels and what she called 'the Herbert pearls' (so named after Michael Herbert, a member of the Pembroke family, who had the finest and whitest teeth in London), she was just about to step into his car, when a fearful noise of quarrelling and a crashing of pots and pans came from the kitchen. 'They're at it again,' she said, 'I'll have to go and cook the dinner. I'll come on later.' She joined him in his box after the first act.

She never lost the habit of early rising and expected her staff to do the same. Because of her matutinal habits, one of her guests nicknamed her 'Rosa de Bonne-heure'. At eight o'clock she called in at the pantry to collect an enormous tea-cup. Wearing a rose-pink flannel dressing-gown, she would then drift into the dining-room where the early birds would be breakfasting. Circling round the room, 'moving haphazardly hither and thither like a fly on a flat pool of water',† she stopped at every table where she spied a tea-pot. Smiling sweetly she would ask if the tea was made just right, saying she would like to taste it to make sure. By pouring a sample from each pot into her cup, she soon filled it to the brim and carried it back to her dressing-room to drink before she started dressing for the day.

In spite of her rough manner with servants and the strange names she bestowed on some of them – 'Alice-where-art-thou?', for instance, was how she addressed a tardy parlour-maid who was for ever disappearing when summoned – she

† Caroll Carstairs, *A Generation Missing*.

did them small kindnesses. Believing in champagne as a pick-me-up, she would often bring a glass of bubbly to a tired house-maid sweeping out a room, and before the 1914 War she used to hold an annual servants' ball to which butlers, valets, cooks, chefs and ladies'-maids from the outside world were invited as well as the friends and relations of her staff. Full evening-dress was worn and she would borrow elegant ball-gowns from Bond Street shops for her Cinderellas. The star of the evening was her head cook, Mrs Charlotte, a willowy Tennysonian beauty, who could easily have been mistaken for a duke's daughter. Some of Rosa's closest friends came to support her on these occasions, including Lord Ribblesdale, who would open the ball with Mrs Charlotte, the two of them making a romantic-looking pair as they waltzed to the lilting strains of 'The Merry Widow' played on the piano and violin. The supper provided was as excellent as any that Rosa prepared for the smart Society dances. There were quails on the menu, of course, and the champagne was vintage.

For many years the Cavendish was served by a barber who called every morning. Mr Jones, of Laurie & Jones, not only used to shave Rosa's clients when they were still in bed, using a cut-throat razor, but he was even able to do so while the sub-ject of the operation slept undisturbed. His fingers seemed to be charged with a healing touch when performing soothing mas-sage on heads suffering from the effects of the night before.

The Cavendish understood hangovers; it probably witnessed more than any other hostelry in London. Here they were dealt with tenderly, and the neighbourhood abounded in chemists who all carried patent remedies. Grays, round the corner, was favoured by Rosa. Their sovereign remedy was the highly efficacious 'Hepatic Granules' which I was told, when I last went there, 'travelled all over the world in diplomatic bags'.

Another establishment which Rosa did her best to encourage was a tailor's shop in Duke Street. All the Amerians staying in the hotel were inveigled by her into having suits made here. 'Used to be So and So's cutter,' she would say, mentioning a Savile Row name. The subject of the tailor was usually brought up in the course of a champagne session in her parlour and it was a strong man who could resist being marched out of the hotel and down the street to be measured. On these occasions the orders were apt to become a little exaggerated. One victim of Rosa's persuasions later reported: 'In my innocence I bought two suits and my resemblance to someone's brother, who Rosa insisted I was, then became complete for no stretch of imagination could conceive that these clothes could ever have been chosen by me,'

There were also several flower shops in the neighbourhood and Rosa was delighted if she found out that one of her richer gentlemen had opened an account at any of these. She would then exercise further Robin Hood tactics, buying flowers which she charged to these wealthy dupes, and sending them to less fortunate friends in hospitals, nursing-homes and prisons.

Not only did she send flowers to prisons, she often visited them in person, and the friendly terms on which she remained with many of the governors sometimes proved helpful to her flock of black sheep.

She also knew all the local prostitutes by name, keeping herself well informed as to each one's medical history, though she preferred her clients to conduct their affairs with amateurs and objected when she found one of them had been with a Jermyn Street girl. 'We'll have to get a doctor to look at your winkle in the morning,' she would say gloomily. Nevertheless at

Christmas the prostitutes were not forgotten and each one would receive a small gift.

Odd channels of philanthropy ran through Rosa's piratical nature, and she would willingly give active help to social and charitable organizations so long as this did not lead to any publicity. She once gave a talk to a Girls' Club in the East End of London, appearing in all the splendour of her sables and black velvet and a toque trimmed with ostrich feathers. Round her neck were the 'Herbert' pearls and pinned on her bosom a beautiful diamond brooch in the shape of a shooting star.

'Look at these furs,' was her opening remark. 'These pearls and this diamond brooch . . . they're all real. Do you know how I got them? Sheer hard work and nothing else. I always wanted them so I worked until I had enough to buy them. Clothes are very important and if you want to get anywhere you must dress as well as you can – they're a good investment.'

This was sound advice and more sympathetic than the speech which Nancy Astor once delivered to an audience of women prisoners: 'You're luckier than I am,' she said. 'You're *wanted* and I'm not.'

In the late twenties, when I was ill in Lady Carnarvon's nursing-home in Portland Place, Rosa came to visit me bearing her traditional gifts of peaches and champagne. On her way out she came face to face with the owner, who also acted as matron. A most attractive woman, Lady Carnarvon was looking particularly beautiful that day, dressed in one of the pastel-coloured, short-sleeved silk dresses she always wore, which reminded one of the tennis courts rather than the operating theatre. Rosa immediately put up her hackles (she often showed hostility towards popular and beautiful women who were not in her circle). 'Just you see young Daphne gets enough to eat,' she snapped, 'she's always making babies.' There was no need for her to worry, however, since the food in the luxurious nursing-home was both plentiful and delicious.

Rosa was a great friend of another famous nursing figure, Sister Agnes Keyser, and regularly visited her at Edward VII Hospital, which Miss Keyser and her sister Fanny had founded in their own house at the beginning of the South African War for officers whose financial means would not permit them to get the necessary treatment elsewhere. The foundation had been the King's idea and the hospital continued under his patronage after the war was over. A trust was set up, and subscriptions poured in from the King's friends, his own name heading the list. Sir Ernest Cassels, Sigmund Newmann, Arthur Sassoon, Lord Burnham, Nathaniel Rothschild, Lord Sandwich, Lord Iveagh and the banker Hambro all subscribed handsomely.

The latter, when asked to make a life subscription, said: 'I hate signing promises, even more than cheques', but did so all the same. Lord Burnham, answering the appeal, wrote: 'Sweet Sister, I shall be delighted to contribute. You are the best woman in the world and I am devotedly yours.' And Baroness Von Echhardstein wrote: 'Agnes darling . . . Fancy feeling uncomfortable about asking me! My dear *clever* little idiot – of course I will . . . Ever your loving little Gracie.'

How the Edwardian sheep all followed the Royal example!

With the formation of this trust a charge of 2s. 6d. a week provided the patients with the services of twenty-seven top-ranking surgeons and physicians. In 1904 the sisters moved the hospital to 9 Grosvenor Gardens, Lord Randolph Churchill's old house, where, among other amenities, there was a roof garden with a view of Buckingham Palace to which King Edward made what the *Daily Mirror* described as 'a brief bright visit' daily.

Sister Agnes had her favourites, usually in the Brigade of Guards and the Household Cavalry, and she amused the King by repeating their gossip to him. As a young woman she had the delicate prettiness and colouring of a Dresden china shepherdess, but her thin firm mouth belied her appearance of fragility. Before she became so completely dedicated to her nursing career she and her sister had led a conventional Society life which centred round the Court. A martinet to her staff, she was infinitely kind to her patients, so long as they conformed to her rules. She made a point of always being present to hold the hand of each man as he went under an anaesthetic. Female visitors to her patients were terrified of her for she treated them with prickly hostility.

It was in her house that King Edward ate the last dinner of his life, when, noticing his unhealthy colour and heavy breathing, she sent for a doctor. The King's death a few days later affected her deeply, and Queen Alexandra, knowing how fond she had been of him, placed a spray of red roses from her on his coffin. She subsequently remained on intimate terms with the royal family and until she died, in 1940, had the key leading from Grosvenor Gardens to Buckingham Palace, where she had the freedom of the royal gardens.

A photograph of this austere figure wearing her matron's uniform looked sternly out of its frame in Rosa's parlour, providing a sharp contrast to some of the rest of the rogues' gallery. Like Rosa, Sister Agnes had always been averse to publicity, and wished for no recognition or reward for her services.

Chapter Thirteen

Rosa's excursions from the Cavendish into the outside world often took the form of an assault, for she ignored such trifles as invitations. Most of all she liked making an impromptu visit to Covent Garden at five o'clock in the morning with a cavalcade of her favourites, still in their evening suits and long ball dresses on the last lap of an all-night jaunt round the town.

The sight of evening dress in the early morning market is something that has quite disappeared. Nobody goes to have breakfast there after a party any more; but in those days the Covent Garden porters were quite used to these elegant intrusions. Rosa would often be in bed and asleep, but to take her to buy flowers had become traditional and so she would be woken up. She wasted no time in dressing and used to slip her sable coat over her nightdress, which trailed behind her, sweeping up old cabbage leaves and broken blossoms in its passage.

Perhaps she cherished nostalgic memories of Covent Garden, which carried her back to the days when she was always up at dawn doing her own marketing, choosing the choicest and youngest vegetables to titillate royal taste-buds. The noises and smells of this familiar stamping-ground made her throw back her head and sniff the air like an old hunter out at grass, listening to the distant sound of a hunting-horn. Her cheeks were flushed pink as the roses she bought in armfuls, while she haggled with the stall holders, swearing and grumbling about present-day prices. Out of sheer devilry, prompted by some market Puck, she could not resist going up to the men carrying tottering piles of baskets on top of their heads and asking them to let her see what they had in the bottom one.

An outing with Rosa was fraught with difficulties from the very start. It was like a game of snakes and ladders and one encountered the first snake in ordering the car – an ancient Daimler even more old-fashioned and regal-looking than Queen Mary's – to come round from the garage at the back of the hotel. Late at night the Cavendish switch-board was often operated by some young man who had failed to pay his bill and was working off the debt through this semi-skilled labour. Sometimes he fell asleep at his post. If the chauffeur could not be contacted, there would then be a procession through the laundry, where anyone who had not been previously warned was liable to doubt his eyes on coming face to face with a small donkey, which had originally been sent to Rosa as a joke by one of her American admirers. For a long time this animal occupied one of the bedrooms, and another of Rosa's American visitors, going into the wrong room after a particularly good dinner, got the shock of his life when he switched on the light and saw the donkey stretched out asleep on the floor.

If the makeshift telephone-operator had succeeded in getting through to the chauffeur, the next snake on the board was to get Rosa dressed and out in time to coincide with the car coming round to the front of the hotel and parking in narrow Jermyn Street.

She particularly enjoyed making a raid on the Gargoyle Club, chiefly because she considered it a challenge to get in without being a member. This club was founded by David Tennant and Harry Walker in 1925. Most of the original members were either painters, writers, poets or musicians, and among them were Augustus John, A. P. Herbert, Compton Mackenzie and Clive Bell.

The Gargoyle seemed to transform ordinary conventional people into Bohemians; on becoming members they even began to dress quite differently. It brought out the dormant Little Billees and Trilbys in county folk. Stiff collars were replaced by open-necked shirts, Heath hats with the diamond regimental badges were discarded for left-bank berets. It was easy to imagine David Tennant's first wife, Hermione Baddeley, kicking her well-turned legs in a can-can à la Goulue, for in its infancy the Gargoyle had a Toulouse-Lautrec atmosphere.

When Rosa took it into her head to come here she rose above the demand that she should at least be accompanied by a member, and flatly refused to sign her name as a visitor. 'Just tell young Tennant I've come to have a look at his place,' she would say as she clanked down the looking-glass-and-brass staircase. At the bottom she would then stand surveying the ballroom whose décor was of a Spanish influence, with coffered ceilings of gold, and walls decorated with scenes copied from the Court of Lions in the Alhambra. Matisse had suggested that it should be walled with mirrors made of slightly imperfect glass which gave a shimmering reflection, and in this Rosa and her picaresque train were multiplied a hundred times.

Here, as everywhere else she went, she stood out from the crowd. Despite her advancing years, she was still said to have the most beautiful neck and shoulders in London; her head was proudly set and she held herself magnificently, walking with an air. She had the presence of royalty, and because of this she seemed more remarkable than anyone else in the room.

She once went to the Gargoyle accompanied by the inevitable Kippy and by Kathleen Lady Drogheda with several other small dogs on a lead. At the bar was Augustus John with that dramatic serpentine figure, the Marquesa Casati, whom he was painting at the time. She was wearing an immense black velvet Merry Widow hat trimmed with cascading rivers of monkey fur and jet. Brian Howard, a character who might have stepped out of an Evelyn Waugh novel, renowned for his epigrams and wicked wit, was goading John. As the discussion warmed up, he emphasized his points with a brandished bottle until the Marquesa's hat, intervening, caught the brunt of the argument and was deluged in a shower of wine, while the canine pets of Lady Drogheda and Mrs Lewis broke into a dog-fight of their own.

When David Tennant objected to this hullabaloo in his artistic club, Rosa was not in the least put out and insisted on being shown the flat below where David and his second wife, Virginia, used sometimes to spend the night. This had been recently decorated, and Rosa, like Queen Mary, always liked to inspect any domestic improvements. Virginia† had a treasured collection of miniscule shells which she had displayed on a tray in a mosaic-like pattern. Feeling peckish and mistaking these for cocktail dainties, Rosa seized a handful, popped them into her mouth and began to crunch them between her teeth.

Her behaviour in restaurants and public places was often eccentric. An inveterate table-hopper, she would wander round causing pandemonium by consciously or unconsciously confusing identities. A complete stranger would be surprised at being greeted with: 'Used to know your grandma . . . Went to Buckingham Palace wearing her false teeth for a brooch.'

She enjoyed talking to the waiters, whom she always remembered, and questioned them about the tips they received, the state of their feet and how many babies they had made.

† Now the Marchioness of Bath.

It sometimes happened that she bore a grudge against one of them, and then she was apt to come out with some such disparaging remark as: 'He's not a bit of good . . . got india-rubber tits.'

Once when she was lunching with Mark Ogilvie Grant at the Berkeley, one of her favourite haunts, a waiter spotted Kippy – a contraband article in this sanctum – half concealed under her trailing skirts. Before he could open his mouth to remonstrate, however, she pitched in with a more than usually deliberate red herring: 'What! Don't skin the tomatoes at the Berkeley Hotel! Send for the manager!'

Throughout her life she was an avid collector, and sales held an irresistible attraction for her. Sometimes, carried away by enthusiasm, she bought some white elephant which was a challenge even to her ingenuity when it came to finding a place for it in the hotel. In this mood she bid for the huge wrought-iron gates from the double marble staircase at Dorchester House. To her surprise they were knocked down to her, and for some time remained in the garden at the back of the Cavendish, until she hit on the idea of constructing from them what looked like an iron cage for some exotic wild beast, but in fact imprisoned the make-shift telephone operator and the temperamental switchboard.

Dorchester House may have held sentimental memories for her, since she also bought many pieces of broken Italianate statuary from its garden, which subsequently lay about the courtyard of the Cavendish on which some of the private suites opened. (Some Caesar's head, a fallen column and cracked urns were dangerous hazards to stumbling feet indiscreetly manœuvring in the dark.) Perhaps she still recalled with nostalgia the days when it was let to an Eastern potentate as an embassy.

Herds of special cows and flocks of sheep and goats were kept in the garden to be slaughtered according to the potentate's religious customs. The death cries of the unfortunate animals heard in Park Lane were mistaken for the yells of concubines, giving rise to rumours of strange sexual orgies – a laughably incongruous notion when one thought of the stately atmosphere of this great London house and its dignified courtier owner, Sir George Holford.

Rosa's method of bidding at a sale must have been very confusing to the auctioneer. Getting over-excited, she would wave her programme in the air as though suffering from some nervous tic; consequently she often found things had been knocked down to her when she was quite unconscious of having bid for them. In this way she was told that she had bought a vicarage. 'Wrap up the parson with it. I might as well take him too,' she said. She was disappointed that this purchase did not include the gift of a living, for she was very partial to her gentlemen of the cloth.

Where she really burgeoned and bloomed, however, was at a wedding. If she wished to go to one, go she did, whether she had received an invitation or not. But sometimes there were straitlaced parents of the bride or groom, who frowned on the idea of the notorious Mrs Lewis's presence as a guest.

On one occasion, at a fashionable wedding at St Margaret's, Westminster, Rosa's name had been struck off the list of guests, but the bride, who loved her, sent off a secret invitation bidding her to come to the reception. There, the guard of honour from the bridegroom's regiment, the Life Guards, had been given, as is usual, a room to themselves and a sumptuous wedding-feast of their own. Rosa, having lost her way, wandered into this room, and sat herself down among the fine strapping men resplendent in breast-plates, plumed helmets, tall boots and swords. She was extremely content with this all-male, handsome and appreciative company, and the troopers were likewise delighted when the aristocratic-looking and beautiful old lady came out with some fruity barrack-room language of her own.

When the bride and bridegroom came in later to drink a toast with them, they found Rosa on top of her form, keeping the men in gales of laughter, her glass brimming with champagne, and her plate piled with *chaud froid* of chicken, strawberries and cream. Before leaving, she invited them all to come and visit her at her hotel. 'Be sure you wear your tin pots and pans, and those red horses' tails in your hats, and I'll fill your gumboots with so much champagne that it won't run out until Easter,' she promised.

The many racing people who stayed at the Cavendish were always welcome with Rosa since she was a born gambler and liked to be given daily tips for her small bet. But she expected the money to be put on for her by these friends 'in the know', and did not think it necessary to pay up if the horse failed to win.

She was once taken to a club where there was a fruit machine for gambling. When told that this was known as 'a one-armed bandit', she was determined to get the better of it. 'You just give me some money,' she said to her escort, 'and see if I bloody well don't get something out of the dratted thing.' After each unsuccessful assault, she went round the bar demanding coins from all and sundry, until there were no more shillings left in pockets or purses. She then tackled the barman: 'Look here,' she said, 'your blinking bandit's busted. Give me one more shilling and I'll show you.' The barman meekly took a shilling from the till, Rosa inserted the coin, and there was a crash of falling silver as the jack-pot rolled out on the floor. 'There! I told you it was broken – got a hole in the bottom,' was her comment, as she hurriedly scooped up the money, stuffed it into her pockets and reticule, and sailed out.

Fortnum and Mason's played a great part in the pattern of her everyday life, and she had made a habit of paying a daily visit to the big grocery store opposite, sometimes carrying a glass from which she sipped while making a purchase, and always with Kippy in her wake. Here she harried and bullied the stately shop-assistants in frock-coats, who winced at her language and turned a craven eye when Kippy lifted his leg on the pyramids of biscuit tins. When one of them timidly drew her attention to her pet's behaviour, she gave him an imperious look and said: 'I know . . . he's my dog,' as if such ownership endowed the animal with *droit de seigneur* over Jermyn Street.

She liked the smell of the expensive groceries, for it must be remembered that she had enjoyed the reputation of being the most extravagant cook in England. The memory of former laurels was revived as she wandered around, sniffing the Stilton cheeses, examining the texture of the Bradenham hams, lingering over the *pâté de foie gras en croute*, and inquiring after the price of caviar and plover's eggs.

On these visits she invariably ran into someone she knew, not always with the happiest results. One afternoon she hailed an attractive, dark and vivacious young woman, whom she seized with that compelling grip of hers which closed like a vice round the wrist of anyone she particularly wished to way-lay. 'You just come over the road with me, dear; I want to talk to you.' At the Cavendish she led her prisoner into the front sitting-room where she ordered her a large glass of milk, and embarked on a long homily on what to eat and drink in order to make a bouncing baby. Coming to the end of her advice, she said: 'Young Charlie's well off with you, Adele.'

'But my name isn't Adele and I'm not having a baby,' the astonished young lady exclaimed.

Rosa had taken her for Lady Charles Cavendish (formerly Adele Astaire).

Some of the best parties within the memory of London were the election ones given by Gordon Selfridge on the roof garden of his big store in Oxford Street. To these he invited every celebrity in town, including, of course, Rosa. Here is a vignette of one given in the thirties:

The guests enter through the bargain basement, virgin territory to Rosa, unaccustomed to such modern emporiums. She is escorted by Lord Charles Cavendish. The lift is controlled by a beautiful tall conductress, whom Mr C. B. Cochran notices with approval. She is dressed like a pantomime highwayman, in a bottle-green coat, cut with a tiered shoulder cape, top boots and a gold-braided tricorne hat, which Rosa wants to try on.

The lift shoots up to the roof garden, disgorging the celebrities. They are greeted by that zoological roar of a party in full swing. Heather Thatcher's cicada rasp rises above Tallulah Bankhead's dark treacly growl.

The guests sit in groups at little tables for supper. Passing one of these a staccato voice with a note of surprise in it rises above the cacophony: it is Lady Cunard's. 'Oh, Mr Robey, I assure you I would not enjoy being the "Only Girl in the World". It would leave me no time in which to go to the Opera.'

Rosa and Charlie Cavendish make an epic entrance together. In their progress through the room, they have captured what is known as a 'running buffet' – and this is exactly what it is doing, for Rosa has started it off by giving it a vigorous shove. The rubber-covered wheels and the weight of the bottles make it move very fast on the sloping floor. Gathering speed, it takes on a wayward life of its own. Charlie gives chase, followed by Rosa flapping her arms and cackling. They never quite manage to catch up with it. The whole room is rocking with laughter – this is funnier than any of the cabaret turns. Finally the escaping buffet careers into a table, upsetting the squeaking Dolly Sisters in a welter of diamonds, feathers and tulle.

As Rosa finally leaves the party a succulent salmon in aspic catches her eye. Picking it up by the tail, she sails out majestically, saying with a wink, 'Just put this down to my account at Fortnum and Mason's.'

Chapter Fourteen

Rosa's attitude towards writers was understandable. She was, openly and frankly, a snob. All her opinions were drawn from those people to whom writers were back-door men, not equals.

In Anthony Glyn's biography of his grandmother he describes how Lady Warwick instructed her as to the correct social etiquette for entertaining in a big country house. She insisted that anyone engaged in the arts, stage, trade or commerce, no matter how well connected, should never be on the invitation list. Edward VII was a close friend of Lady Warwick's, and her opinion would certainly be one which Rosa respected.

The fact that Lord Ribblesdale had written books, she dismissed as an aristocratic whim; besides, 'putting things down' like that stopped him from getting the hump. As to young Shane Leslie, coming from such a nice family and all, well, the least said about those novels of his the better.

Evelyn Waugh finally cooked the writers' goose as far as Rosa was concerned with his portrait of 'Lottie Crump' and 'Shepheard's Hotel', and after *Vile Bodies* appeared she obstinately refused to discriminate between a writer and a gossip columnist (unless the latter happened to be a lord). 'You can't trust them a yard – put you in a book for tuppence, cut your throat for five bob and your corns for half a crown.' Her dislike for literary practitioners became an obsession with her, and she began to imagine that any man under fifty whom she did not happen to like must be a writer.

Mr Waugh's intriguing description of 'Shepheard's' had the immediate effect of attracting fellow-authors to the Cavendish, who often stayed there without Rosa realizing their profession, for she very rarely read a book. But although Rosa had no intellectual interests she respected what she called 'book learning' and a man such as Augustine Birrell for whom she had cooked before she became owner of the Cavendish, was treated with awe and respect. He was a man of critical taste, a connoisseur and a bibliophile. His profession was the law and he also represented a Scottish constituency in the House of Commons. Rosa looked up to Birrell as a sage since he wrote essays on learned subjects and eschewed the vulgar novel. When she cooked for his dinner-parties she was impressed with the attention he gave to every detail of the arrangements. Above all she admired the punctuality and precision with which he ordered his life, for although she did not apply these virtues in the running of her hotel, she recognized their merit.

If a writer happened to be American, she modified her views to a certain extent; for to her all Americans were sacrosanct, enthroned in a dollar aristocracy of their own. Perhaps that is why she raised no objection to Thornton Wilder and Carl van Vechten, both of whom visited the Cavendish in the twenties, nor even to the latter's vignette of herself in his book, *Parties*.

Rosa also made an exception of Sir James Barrie, for he was a friend of Sir William Eden and a knight to boot. Besides, she liked Pauline Chase, one of the early Peter Pans, who used to stay at the Cavendish where Otto Kahn sent her so many flowers that she did not miss the ones Rosa purloined from her and dispatched to prisons and hospitals.

Pauline Chase was much admired and her clothes were always remarked upon in the Press. In 1906 *Modern Society* describes her as wearing 'a black *crêpe de Chine* dress relieved by a little chemisette and under-sleeves of white-embroidered lawn, while round the crown of her black hat was folded a band of Sèvres blue silk which at the left side was drawn into a huge *chou*, the other side being occupied by a big bunch of pink roses set round with glossy leaves.'

In 1932 Aldous Huxley and his first wife stayed at the hotel and in a recent letter to me he described his visit:

'It was like staying in a run-down country house – large comfortable rooms, but everything shabby and a bit dirty. We were not bibulous, so must have been a disappointment to Rosa Lewis. However, she put up with us. Once, I remember, a young man in what the lady novelists call "faultless evening dress", top hat and all, came swaying into our bedroom at almost 2.30 a.m., and had to be pushed out. How sad, but how inevitable, that the hotel should now be doomed to destruction.'

Cyril Conolly, and his first wife, Jean, also stayed in the hotel at one time, but avoided Rosa's court circle – a wise move if he wanted to work, for once she had taken a fancy to anyone all privacy was disrupted and it then became necessary to lock bedroom doors in order to prevent the intrusion at all hours of bodies, vile and otherwise, led by Rosa demanding yet another party. She was always drifting 'upstairs and downstairs and in my lady's chamber', glass in hand, effecting introductions, for she liked people to make friends in her hotel.

To get the essence of the Cavendish one had to be 'in the Club'; and if a writer could stand the pace and keep his wits about him, there was much to observe from this vantage point. Joseph Bryan III used to stay here in the early thirties when he was a young journalist on the *New Yorker*. He wrote a brilliant profile of Rosa. For a long time she thought he was 'someone else's brother', but finally he became a favourite in his own right and she gave him a very handsome suite for about £2 a day, which was less than half its usual rental.

One morning he was lying soaking in his bath when the door of the suite opened and he heard Rosa's voice showing some visitors round. Paralysed with fright, he was unable to get out of the bath and bolt the door. 'The sitting-room,' he heard Rosa say, 'and the bedroom, and the bath . . .' The door was flung wide. There stood Rosa with an elderly couple, staring at him in the bath. She continued imperturbably, 'Five guineas a day, the young chap not included.'

A few nights later, at the soup-course of a white-tie dinner, he was violently shaken by an onslaught of malaria, contracted on a recent shooting trip to Kenya, and by the time he had made his way back to the Cavendish he was on the edge of delirium. There was a young Dutch baroness also staying in the hotel, who had just finished training as a nurse. He has only the vaguest recollection of her helping him upstairs, undressing him, putting him into bed and dosing him with quinine. But he remembers clearly finding her in an arm-chair in his room in the morning. The fever passed quickly, as it does with malaria; he thanked the baroness and sent her flowers. But when his week's bill came in it was for £78. He protested vigorously, but was told by Rosa that when one of her young ladies spent the night with one of her young gentlemen, the young gentleman automatically assumed the young lady's bill. He flatly refused to do so.

When his profile appeared, hundreds of Americans sent Rosa copies of the *New Yorker*. But although it was written with the greatest affection, she resented it, for she was touchy and nervous of publicity. In fact she was so furious with the author that she wrapped up all the copies of the magazine she had received in lead-foil paper, and kept the bundle in readiness for his next visit when she intended to balance it on top of his bedroom door, as a booby trap, to fall on his head. When the time came, however, she forgave him and refrained from breaking his neck.

George Millar, the author of *Horned Pigeon, Unicorn Gates*, and other books, was one of the few writers with whom Rosa had an entirely happy relationship. He first met her when he was 17. He had then left Loretto to take the Littlego at Cambridge and was passing through London with a dashing school-friend who said, 'Let's go to the Cavendish. I bet Rosa Lewis knows your old man.' He was right.

George was a very shy young man, but Rosa understood such people and with her he immediately felt at ease. A few years later, he quarrelled with his family over a girl he wanted to marry, left home and came to stay at the Cavendish: a move which appalled his mother. Finally he eloped with the girl and for a time was cut off parentally. Rosa came to the rescue and lent the star-crossed lovers her cottage at Jevington. Here George was able to write in the greenhouse, while his girl-friend did the cooking on a Primus stove in the sitting-room.

In a letter to his mother, Rosa said, 'Don't worry about young George, he had best get it out of his system. Best if he doesn't have to marry her, though she is a very nice girl. In any event Edith and I will keep him safe for you.' Later on George's mother came to know and like Rosa, whom she admired for the wisdom she had shown in regard to her son's love affair.

Rosa's affection for George was even proof against his work-ing in Fleet Street, and in loyalty he never wrote a word about her. When his girl-friend fell ill, Rosa trundled round at all hours to the bed-sitting-room where they were living, bringing doctors, invalid delicacies, wine, flowers and company.

After the war, in which George served as a clandestine agent in enemy-occupied territory, he again stayed at the Cavendish, where he wrote all day in a corner of the dining-room. Rosa would watch him with a bemused expression, but she never took his writing seriously.

A further illustration of Rosa's attitude towards writers in general was described by John Foster in an early issue of *Lilliput*. A young man named Toby Sloan-Onslow used to stay at the Cavendish when he came to London on a periodical binge. He had plenty of money, and was high-spirited and extrovert in the way Rosa liked most. During one of these jaunts he met an old Oxford friend named Vincent Hawkins, for whom things had gone badly wrong – in the same week he had lost both his job and his wife, who had run off with one of his friends.

Toby Sloan-Onslow arranged for him to stay the night at the Cavendish, where he hoped he might be able to help him forget his troubles for a while. Next morning he took him into Rosa's parlour to buck him up with champagne before lunch, but for some unknown reason she at once took against the newcomer. They didn't stay long, and Toby, thinking she was in a temporary bad mood, decided he would try again before dinner. This time it was even worse, and Vincent, out of nerves, sat on Kippy, who was invisible under a sofa cushion. Halfway through the second bottle of champagne Rosa said. 'Here, Toby, does that friend of yours think he is staying here tonight?'

'Yes, Rosa,' replied Tony. 'You see, he's got nowhere else to go. His wife's left him and the poor chap needs cheering up badly, and you're the person to do that if anyone is.'

'Well, I don't like him,' said Rosa, clacking her teeth together and ignoring the flattery. 'He's a writer and I won't have writers here. I'm not surprised his wife left him. I expect he tried to put her in a book.'

Toby did his best to make her realize that his friend was certainly not a writer, but she obstinately stuck to her opinion and to the decision that he was not to stay in the hotel. That night, when Toby and Vincent returned very late, they found that she had left instructions with Moon that there was no room in the hotel for Mr Sloan-Onslow's friend. Toby told Moon that he was prepared to take full responsibility with Mrs Lewis, who would certainly have changed her mind by the morning. Meanwhile his friend could share his room.

But in the morning Rosa was still adamant.

Toby Sloan-Onslow was now thoroughly annoyed with her, thinking she had been unkind and unreasonable, and he decided to take up the challenge and defeat her veto by hook or by crook. During the next week he applied himself with great ingenuity to smuggling Vincent in and out of the Cavendish, concentrating with an intentness he had rarely shown before.

It was an exhausting process since Vincent could not attempt to reach the sanctuary of Toby's rooms before at least half past one in the morning, when Rosa might start going to bed. Toby's first idea was a rope-ladder hung outside his bedroom window, which looked out on the garage, but another guest saw a figure climbing in and reported it to Rosa, who found the ladder and confiscated it next day. Toby then made elaborate plans for Vincent to be carried into the hotel in a laundry basket, but this ruse was discovered through the noise of the party in Toby's room celebrating the success of the manœuvre. Rosa then issued the order that all laundry baskets should be opened in her presence.

Vincent then managed to burrow his way in through a coal-hole. Another time, he walked straight through the hall of the hotel carrying a tray of muffins on his head and ringing a bell. On yet another occasion he succeeded in slipping in behind a band which had been engaged to play at a party, his face hidden by the big drum he was carrying. There were many other abortive attempts, but he was always detected and thrown out. After being turned away three times in one night, the friends lost heart.

For some time Toby avoided the Cavendish, and then, unable to keep up the feud any longer, dropped in to see Rosa. He fully intended to avoid the subject of Vincent, but she could not resist making a Parthian fling. 'Well . . . we haven't seen anything of that writer friend of yours for a long time. Good riddance to bad rubbish,' she said, chuckling triumphantly.

This was too much for Toby, who decided to make a last desperate attempt. He went outside, then telephoned to the Cavendish in the name of the Portuguese Naval Attaché, asking for a room to be reserved for a Commander de Sousa. Meanwhile Vincent was tracked down and taken to Clarksons where he was rigged out in a naval uniform, false whiskers and a beard. The disguise was complete. At midnight he went round to the hotel, where Rosa received him most civilly. Toby came in later and was introduced to the Commander. Champagne was ordered, and other people joined the party. But it soon became apparent that Rosa had taken one of her unpredictable dislikes to the Portuguese commander, who was amusing everyone else telling stories in broken English. Getting up she stumped to the door and called for Moon.

'Does that Greek admiral think he's staying here?' she asked. Moon replied that 43 had been booked for Commander de Sousa by the Portuguese Naval Attaché. 'Well, I'm not going to have him. You can tell them we're full up. He looks like a bloody writer. They ought to know I won't have writers here.'

Rosa had more respect for painters, finding them better spenders than writers. Besides, they were often knighted, like Sir Alfred Munnings and Sir William Orpen, both habitués of the Cavendish.

Orpen was a Dubliner, a character of much light and shade, with many friends and enemies. As a boy he once jumped on an engine and pulled a lever to satisfy his curiosity: the engine started. Lord Castlerosse, describing this incident in the *Sunday Express*, commented: 'This was rather his system in conversation. He would say things to start something.' One can understand how he hit it off so well with Rosa.

Sickert had been the friend of Sir William Eden, as well as his ally in the Whistler quarrel. Sargent had painted the wonderful portrait of Lord Ribblesdale. Both of them therefore were given the freedom of Rosa's parlour and were welcome in the Elinor Glyn. As for Augustus John, he had the kind of vitality that she most admired. He often came to the Cavendish with Sylvia Gough, in whose divorce he figured as co-respondent, together with Maurice de Rothschild and Mr Bertrand Nedeker. Like most Edwardians, Rosa disapproved of divorce, but if it had to happen she preferred the co-respondents to be rich, famous or well born. Sylvia's had come up to scratch on all counts.

Augustus John was also a great friend of Margot Asquith, whose high spirits and blade-sharp wit enchanted Rosa. She had known her for many years, since she often visited her brother-in-law, Lord Ribblesdale, when he was living in the hotel. Rosa was also fond of one of John's models and used to make bets as to how soon she would strip to the buff, and 'cut capers like Isadora Duncan'.

The best portrait of Rosa – a charcoal drawing in the manner of Sargent – was done by a young American, Ned Murray, who died while he was in his early thirties. But the picture of her which caused the greatest sensation when it was exhibited at the Academy in the mid-twenties was the work of the painter Guevara. Commenting on it, a contemporary newspaper reported:

'The portrait of Mrs Lewis of the Cavendish Hotel depicting a lady reclining on a lovely sofa, her skirt catching the firelight and her expressive face turned tensely towards the painter, makes the most exciting contribution.'

Sir Alfred Munnings earned her undying gratitude when she telephoned him saying she was unable at the last moment to obtain tickets for the Chelsea Arts Ball. At this time he was President of the Royal Academy. Immediately he sent a messenger with a slip of paper on which was scrawled: 'Please admit Mrs Rosa Lewis and party. Alfred Munnings.'

Rosa, wearing a bearskin which had been abandoned at the Cavendish by some absent-minded Guards officer, sailed in free, a rival in beauty to Lady Diana Cooper who was similarly accoutred.

Chapter Fifteen

When I married my first husband, Henry Weymouth, in 1927, Rosa and Edith were guests at the wedding, celebrated at St Martin-in-the-Fields, and came on to the reception held at Dorchester House – the last party to be given there before it was pulled down to make way for the Dorchester Hotel. Rosa was conspicuous among all other guests, in her white Busvine coat and skirt – the one she usually sported at Cowes Regatta – and a dark green Homburg hat trimmed with a collection of small stuffed birds perched on the crown. 'You've got to make a boy, dear,' she repeated over each successive glass of champagne.

But my first child was a girl: a disappointment to Rosa who had a Chinese approach towards daughters. In one of her albums I found the following note, written by my former husband in erratic handwriting, clearly indicating an over-celebration of the event: 'Dear Mrs Lewis, This is Henry Weymouth, the husband of Daphne Vivian, whose mother you loved. We have just had a baby daughter. We are going to call her Caroline. Please come and see her soon.'

It is signed Weymouth and Stavordale.

Harry Stavordale,* is Caroline's godfather; he and Henry had dined together the night after her birth. His own first child, born several years after ours, was also a girl. His cousin Robin Castlereagh,† and a friend of his, John Erne,‡

* Now the Earl of Ilchester.
† Later the Marquess of Londonderry.
‡ Lord Erne, killed in the last war.

likewise became the fathers of girls on the very same day, October 12th, when most of their friends were out of London, either shooting grouse up north or travelling abroad.

Rosa at once sent them a telegram, bidding them to come to the Cavendish to celebrate with champagne. She was waiting on the steps to greet them. 'Well . . . You've all had daughters,' she said, 'You'll have to put them back. I'd have given you a cherrybum each if they'd been sons. As it is you'll have to be content with a pint.' In spite of the sex of these babies, however, a jeroboam was opened.

To go to the Cavendish after any ceremony or celebration connected with the royal family seemed the fitting thing to do. King George V's Jubilee was celebrated in London with flags and singing and dancing on the streets, while crowds stood all day outside Buckingham Palace cheering themselves hoarse as King George and Queen Mary made countless appearances on the balcony. In this jingoistic mood Henry and I went round to Rosa's. We found the place decked with bunting, supporting the biggest and oldest Union Jack in Jermyn Street. Rosa was sitting in the front parlour, holding court. The best champagne was flowing and over and over again we drank the King's health. Next day we received a postcard written in Rosa's round generous scrawl:

'Dear Daphne and Henry,
    You really gave me a Jubilee cheer. You are champagne to Society, both of you. All my love

Rosa.

PS. One million tons of luck.'

Rosa in her big-hearted way always thought in millions and billions. Lord Ilchester still treasures the cheque she sent him in 1932.

Pay to Bearer
the sum of one billion pounds. Thick gold pounds.
                                        Rosa Lewis.

The Cavendish was also the accepted meeting place before going to a royal wedding. On these occasions Rosa always looked a little envious since she enjoyed weddings of any sort and would have given anything to be invited to a royal one. But she voiced her feelings only once, when, seeing us all leave her to go to the Duke of Kent's wedding to Princess Marina, she said with a toss of her head, 'We have royal weddings *here* every day.'

A Court ball at Buckingham Palace, too, was often followed by a visit to the Cavendish. Rosa would be woken up and appeared in a trice, slipping her 'sables of sin' over her bishop-sleeved lawn nightdress. Any occasion connected with the monarchy merited her best champagne, which compared favourably with the royal wine that had been served at the supper.

There was one particular summer dawn which broke through the windows of the Elinor Glyn room to the tune of a Strauss waltz being played on the piano by Sir Richard Sykes. ('Used to call your grandmother "Nostrils",' Rosa said when greeting him.) Everyone started dancing again in the grey light of the breaking day. The first rays of the rising sun were reflected in diamonds, sapphires, emeralds and rubies, as jewel-bedecked beauties, their tiaras by this time slightly askew, waltzed with tall uniformed figures, gold-braided and be-medalled, resplendent as cock-pheasants. Rosa watched and nodded approvingly, but put her foot down when Henry suggested a game of darts with swords.

Later in the morning, when the charwomen appeared with

their mops and pails, they found a tiara, a Hussar's shako, and a bearskin or two, which they tried on in front of the Chinese Chippendale looking-glass.

My brother, Tony Vivian,† as a young man, was always in hot water with my very strict father. After leaving Eton he had gone to Seale Hayne Agricultural College where he led a minor rebellion and burnt an effigy of the headmaster. He was immediately expelled, whereupon my father decreed that he must travel steerage to Canada and get his agricultural knowledge by working on a farm as a labourer.

My grandmother, Mrs Harry McCalmont, and my father had barely spoken to each other since my mother's divorce. Our outings with her were rationed, and, as we grew older, we were never allowed to stay with her. She now realized that this was the moment to have a tilt at the enemy and came stamping into the arena with the announcement that she would pay for Tony's passage to Canada, where he could live with friends of hers and work on their farm. My brother was then told that he must choose between my grandmother and my father. He chose my grandmother.

His apprenticeship on the Canadian farm lasted under a year. One afternoon in London, I read on a newspaper poster: 'Mounted Police Search Rockies for Peer's Missing Heir'. Tony had run away. The search went on for three weeks and he was finally found in Montreal. Granny McCalmont as usual came to the rescue, forgave him as she always did, and paid his passage home.

My brother and I have always been very close to each other and I was anxious to find an immediate solution as to where he should live. While he was in Canada I had married Henry,

† Now Lord Vivian.

whom my grandmother adored. Between us we managed to persuade her to allow Tony to stay at the Cavendish, where Rosa, I felt sure, would take him under her wing. On looking back, I cannot imagine however we managed to convince her that this was a good plan, for she always disapproved of my going to see Rosa, holding it against her that General Cowans (my grandmother's great love) used to give dinner-parties there for other beautiful ladies in the private suites.

There was also the trouble that Granny had had with James Stanard, her butler, to whom the Cavendish was a forbidden paradise to which he was always escaping. James had risen from being an under-footman. He was my first love when I was very small. It was ecstasy for me to be carried upstairs on his shoulders, and I took advantage of this position to put my arms round his neck. Although he had been a smart footman, he deteriorated with promotion but still remained in my grandmother's employment for many years. She treated him as the cross she had to bear, and sighed whenever she mentioned his name, accusing him of all sorts of crimes I am sure he never committed – he was merely sloppy, lazy and a trifle light-fingered. To my brother and myself he was a favourite comic figure. Whenever Tony did not get on with his lessons as he should have done, James would say, 'Master Tony will not con-cen-ertrate.'

My grandmother was a great traveller and spent much of her time abroad, during which James, unbeknown to her, would take a part-time job at the Cavendish. Rosa was as fascinated by my grandmother and her life as James was by the life at the hotel, so this arrangement was agreeable to both of them. It continued until Granny found out about this double employment and forbade him to work for Mrs Lewis. But although he kept away from the Cavendish for a time, he could never resist its allure for long.

Bearing all this in mind it is amazing that my grandmother agreed to pay for my brother's bed and board at Rosa's.

At this time Tony had begun working as a journalist. This did not worry Rosa since his job was connected only with theatrical news. He was 22, and very attracted by women, who found an equal attraction in him. A middle-aged Argentinian lady, who for many years had been the mistress of Alfonso XIII of Spain, took a particular fancy to him. She was extremely rich and enjoyed spending money at the Cavendish. Rosa liked her enormously and so my brother was used as a bait to attract her to the hotel, but he, having a predilection for younger, theatrical fish, began to avoid her ever-extending octopus tentacles.

One night when he had retired to bed, he was woken up by Steffany with an order from Rosa to get up and go to a party in the Argentinian·lady's house; she had sent her car, which was waiting outside. Tony refused, but Steffany was sent back with instructions to see that he got up at once. 'Tell Mrs Lewis this is an hotel,' Tony protested. 'You live in an hotel and you should be allowed to sleep in peace in an hotel.'

'Hotel!' squeaked Steffany. 'Dis is not an hotel. Dis is an insane asylum!'

While Tony was living in 'dis insane asylum' he fell in love with a young married woman. As a schoolgirl, years before, she had had a slight squint and wore wire-framed spectacles. Wriggling as she talked, like an ingratiating puppy, ever-eager to play, she was always slightly out of breath and looked as if she had come down the chimney backwards (which she was quite capable of doing).

This ink-stained imp had now developed into the most

fascinating feline creature, with a lovely slinky figure, soignée and beautifully dressed; and to add to her allure she had just the right kind of stutter. Tony met her at a theatrical party, was bowled over by her and forthwith brought her back to the Cavendish, where he found Rosa had gone to bed and Steffany was the only person about. He asked for one of the best suites to be opened and ordered a magnum of champagne to be served there. Steffany refused to produce the champagne, but was finally persuaded to open up a room on the understanding that Tony would take full responsibility and make it all right with Mrs Lewis next morning.

My brother and his girl-friend were woken up by Rosa in a towering fury. 'I'm telephoning your Granny to come round here and see what you've got up to,' she said, and put this threat into immediate execution. My grandmother did not appear in person but sent, as an envoy, her embarrassed secretary – a spinster who had led a sheltered life – with marching orders for Tony to pack, leave the Cavendish and report immediately to her at 74 South Audley Street.

The girl was later on divorced and Tony was cited as co-respondent, but the necessary evidence was not obtained from the Cavendish.

It was a hard job persuading my grandmother to overlook this episode, but I succeeded, pointing out it had nothing to do with Rosa, who had been so indignant with my brother that before he left she had thrown his new bowler-hat out into Jerymn Street, where a taxi had run over it. However, she eventually forgave him and he was received back into the fold.

Another young girl to whom Tony paid court was golden-haired, turquoise-eyed Victoria Oliphant, one of the pretty Society girls who used to drop into the hotel to have drinks with Rosa. She was then working as a *vendeuse* in Lady Victor

Paget's dress-shop. Rosa did not approve of Tony's attempt to monopolize her. 'Look here, Tony,' she told him, 'give the others a chance to talk to young Victoria. You're wasting your time if you think there's any bed and breakfast there.'

'Perhaps that's why I like her so much,' Tony replied.

He and Victoria eventually married.

When my grandmother died, Rosa called at 74 South Audley Street with flowers. James opened the door and Rosa persuaded him to allow her to go upstairs to have a last look at his mistress. After this I was not surprised to hear that James had come to a sticky end, for Rosa ceased to employ him when she found the spoons and the drink disappeared whenever he was at the Cavendish. Alas! poor James – he was run over by a bus.

My children all grew up to love Rosa and the Cavendish, which with its passages, corridors and secret entrances provided the perfect ambience for hide and seek (other less innocent characters finding it ideal for a more sophisticated version of the game).

We usually stayed with Rosa for a few days at the end of the holidays. During one of these visits, my second son, Christopher, aged 10, who had received a succession of bad reports from his private school, was forbidden as a punishment to go to the circus. There was a children's luncheon-party beforehand, throughout which Christopher put on a devil-may-care act, which did not fool Rosa and Edith, who were greatly distressed. As I left Edith whispered to me, 'Don't worry, dear, we'll see he has a good time here' – which indeed he did, for the Cavendish was a circus in its own right.

Chapter Sixteen

I never knew the Cavendish in its gastronomic heyday. After the twenties Rosa made no further personal effort with her cooking. She had run her race and won. Food no longer interested her and she did not even seem to derive any pleasure from eating – a penalty perhaps that most great cooks have to face in the end. In her parlour only Escoffier's photograph reminded one of her former prowess, as black velvet and sandwiches replaced set meals and well-chosen menus.

The hotel was now looked upon as a 'period piece'. A third generation of Americans was making pilgrimages to see Rosa Lewis, who ranked with such sights as Nelson's column and the Tower of London. She had become a part of history. When a party was given at the Cavendish, it was usually from the desire to evoke a 'Vile Bodies' atmosphere or to complete the circle and return in spirit to the naughty nineties when Rosa was in her early bloom. Besides, the ambience of the hotel provided an escape from the present and a change from fashionable and conventional entertaining. For these reasons Lord Berners chose the Cavendish in which to entertain the Russian Ballet.

My stepcousin, Robin Wilson,† also preferred it to smarter hotels and gave many parties there. His friends, Jock Whitney and Sir John Millbanke, who were both at Cambridge with

† Killed in the last war on active service in France with the Leicestershire Yeomanry.

him, were often his co-hosts. All three played polo, and the mere sound of this word was a passport to Rosa's heart.

With the Cavendish of the thirties I associate the seductive voice and the piano-playing of 'Hutch'. Robin Wilson told me that he once invited a beautiful but hitherto unyielding lady to dine with him in one of Rosa's suites. For the occasion he engaged Hutch to play, in an adjoining room, songs such as 'I've got you under my skin', 'Body and Soul' and 'Just one of those things'. They worked like a love potion.

Another cousin, Sir Michael Duff, gave a dance for which Rosa opened all the best rooms. She was delighted with this evening for, besides all the *jeunesse dorée*, Michael had invited many impressive old ladies, some of whom must have been greatly intrigued at setting foot inside the Cavendish for the first time and meeting the notorious Mrs Lewis, who ended the evening sitting on a small sofa with her arms around Alice Lady Salisbury and her friend Lady Desborough, both revelling in Rosa's salty reminiscences.

In the early thirties, when Henry and I were staying with Lord Beaverbrook in London at Stornoway House, we were invited to a party at the Cavendish given by Aly Khan and Michael Beary. Lord Beaverbrook's son, Max Aitken, then in his teens, had also been asked, but old Max did not wish him to go. The party proved to be one of the best, with an extremely mixed bag of guests and Hutch at the piano, and during it I ran into young Max, who asked me to promise not to tell his father that I had seen him there.

Next morning I was riding with the older Max, who wanted to know all about the previous night's dance. I told him the gossip and any incidents that I had remembered, withholding the details of his son's presence with some difficulty. Point-blank he turned on me and asked, 'Was my son there?' 'No, Max,' I replied and cantered off briskly down the Row. When he caught up we subsided into a trot, and then he said: 'Daphne, you've missed the best story of all,' and told me of a very funny incident that I had forgotten to give in my report. It was early morning and I wondered how he could be so well primed with the news. 'Who told you that, Max?' I asked. 'My son,' was the reply. 'I saw him before we came out today.'

When Rosa made the anonymous offer, in 1925, which purchased Castle Rock, Cowes, she out-bid the Royal Yacht Squadron who were most anxious to buy the property and turn it into a ladies' annex – an arrangement which would have been greatly appreciated by the female guests since there were no cloakroom facilities available to them.

Castle Rock consisted of a small house, a garden and a separate ballroom – the latter, known as the 'Pavilion', being all that was left of Hippisley House which had once belonged to George III – and Rosa must have paid a very large sum for it, because she had to raise her bids to astronomical heights before the Yacht Squadron would give way to this unknown rival who seemed determined to acquire the property at all costs. It was a shock to them when the anonymous purchaser turned out to be Mrs Lewis of the Cavendish Hotel.

Rosa carried on a perpetual feud with her neighbours of the R. Y. S. Like her friend Sir William Eden, she relished a good quarrel and derived great pleasure from writing insulting letters to the Squadron and threatening legal action over the lavatories they were proposing to build in her garden. 'They won't let me walk on their old lawn and yet they have the cheek to think they can build their bloody W.Cs in my rose-bed,' she exclaimed. In spite of this vendetta, however, she had many friends in the Squadron who visited her house, and she was also entertained by the more broadminded residents to luncheon and dinner.

Lady Kathleen Curzon Herrick once told me how Rosa at one of these luncheon-parties watched the egg dish being handed round the table and refused by all the female guests (it was in the days of earnest slimming when women wished to look like greyhounds). Unable to tolerate these manners, Rosa burst out: 'I can't have this, that dish took four hours to prepare. I'm a cook and I know.' She made every one of them eat it.

No one knows why Rosa wanted a house at Cowes. Was it because it fitted in with the Edwardian tradition? Or because she cherished nostalgic feelings for halycon days spent on the Kaiser's yacht, the *Hohenzollern*, and Harry McCalmont's magnificent boat, *Giralda II*? There were many photographs of yachts and yachtsmen in her parlour, including an enchanting daguerreotype of my trim little grandmother in a wasp-waisted boating costume with leg-of-mutton sleeves and brass buttons, a yachting cap perched squarely on her Alexandra fringe, with a little girl dressed in a sailor blouse and a big round straw hat – my mother.

The only reason Rosa ever gave for the purchase of Castle Rock was that 'Cowes needed livening up'. This she certainly managed to achieve, and in her house there were many strange figures, who would never have been seen in Cowes had they not been guests at Mrs Lewis's. Members of the Squadron, such as Lord Birkenhead, were delighted to find they could play roulette with her. There were also exceptional dinner-parties, when Rosa returned to the kitchen range and cooked the dinner. She liked to invite girls to stay whom she thought were 'on the shelf'. 'Just you come to Cowes,' she said, 'and we'll find you a husband for sure.' But in spite of all her good intentions she never succeeded in her match-making.

In her garden there was a sort of observation post which she called 'my yachting box', from which she could see the Squadron landing stage. During the Regatta she would sit there, the piratical captain of her motley crew, mocking her friends as they disembarked from smart yàchts, and jeering all the more if they were accompanied by hoity-toity wives.

When Rosa first began to 'brighten up Cowes', Poppy Baring was the acknowledged belle of the regatta. Although she had been christened Azalea, she was always called 'Poppy' and no other name could have suited her exotic, velvet-eyed beauty so well. Her parents, Sir Godfrey and Lady Baring, lived at Nubia House, Cowes, where the Prince of Wales and Prince George were frequent guests. Poppy was connected with everything that Rosa thought most worth while; she regarded her as a symbol of attraction. For years she used to say when persuading people to stay on a little longer at any gathering, 'Don't go yet . . . Poppy Baring will be coming.' This formula was used at Cowes, at the Cavendish, in the Ritz and the Berkeley, and on any person whom she wished to delay. It often worked.

Rosa was delighted whenever Poppy and her amusing sister Viola made secret visits to her at Castle Rock – visits which had to be clandestine since Sir Godfrey and Lady Baring had forbidden them. The house was approached by a path where the bases of buried champagne bottles formed a cobbled walk. After each party the path grew longer. Poppy and Viola, strolling demurely beside their parents on the Yacht Squadron lawn were often embarrassed by Rosa bawling a greeting at them from her 'yachting box', recalling some incident of the previous night in her house and reminding the girls that they had helped add more bottles to her path.

The ballroom below Castle Rock was finally bought by the

Yacht Squadron in 1929 and turned into a ladies' annex, at last providing the necessary cloakrooms. Before she sold it, popular Dudley Ward, who was one of Rosa's champions in the Yacht Squadron, gave a ball there, and Rosa took on the catering, exerting all her old skill. It was said to have been the best ball that was ever held at Cowes.

Castle Rock, like Jevington, was always available as a sanctuary for Rosa's friends, and hotel favourites at a loose end would find themselves whisked off to Cowes before they could say 'Veuve Clicquot'. In this way, a young man called Jackie Pringle and a friend of his, Victor Harvey (both of them at Sandhurst), were hustled from the Cavendish into her vintage Daimler and found themselves heading for Cowes and the regatta. At this time Rosa was at the height of her vendetta with the Squadron and in spite of the heat of the day she was wearing her fur toque. This was always a danger signal, rather like the *sans culottes* donning the Phrygian cap.

On the way down she seemed to be brooding over something, and on the ferry she kept muttering 'They're all off their heads at Cowes, the whole blooming lot of them.' There was a picnic basket in the car filled with the bottles of Krug 1921 which were all empty by the end of the journey. When they arrived Moon was waiting for them with a grudging greeting. Rosa ordered more champagne to be brought out to the yachting box. There they sat, drinking quietly, tired after the journey in the heat of the day, when Rosa suddenly raised her head and sniffed the air belligerently.

'What are those bastards doing on the other side of the wall?' she demanded. 'That old Bitching and Tossing and all the stuck-up lot of them?'

She pulled a chair forward, stood on it and looked over.

Whatever it was she saw annoyed her even further, and she turned round with blue Very lights flaring in her eyes.

'Moon!' she shouted. 'Go upstairs and bring me a po from every bedroom. I'm going to throw them at these swollen-headed snobs. Put a penny inside each one of them too.'

Moon, looking more disapproving than ever, delivered this equipment and battle-stations were taken up in the 'yachting box'. Rosa launched the first missile, while the two young soldiers remained cravenly in the background with Edith who was overcome with giggles. One after the other she lobbed and tossed the chinaware over the wall.

'That'll match your silly faces,' she chortled, pitching the final pot.

There was a crash and tinkle of breaking crockery which sounded as if she had scored a bull's eye in the middle of a tea table.

'Stuffy bunch of hypocrites,' she sniffed. 'Well . . . we've had enough of them for today.'

George Kinnaird went to stay with her at Castle Rock and help her prepare for the ball she gave there in honour of King George V's Jubilee. This party went with a riotous swing and even she was a little tired afterwards. In order to get back to the Cavendish in time for the celebrations in London, she did not travel by car, as was her usual custom, but flew back. Unused as she was to this mode of travel, the flight left her quite unmoved, and after she and George had drunk a bottle of champagne from tulip-shaped goblets, she fell asleep. When she woke up she did not realize they had taken off and landed. 'When are we going to start?' she asked.

Over and over again life with Rosa fell into an Alice-through-the-Looking-Glass pattern. On this flight the other passengers included even a King's Messenger. Rosa's conversation surprised him, and one can imagine him with hare's ears pricked to catch the erratic flow of her talk, and surely he should have been called 'Haigha' (pronounced to rhyme with Mayor) and must have struck an 'Anglo-Saxon attitude' as he offered her a ham sandwich from the diplomatic bag hanging round his neck.

Chapter Seventeen

Magistrate: 'Is your name Rosa Lewis?'
Mrs Lewis: 'And why not?'

This was Rosa's attitude whenever she appeared in the law courts. On these occasions she made an impressive appearance: very much the Duchess of Jermyn Street, wearing her pearls and sables. Completely serene and unselfconscious, she made a good impression on judge and jury. The witness-box held no terrors for her and I believe she even enjoyed herself in it for she always liked showing off a bit.

After clients of the Cavendish had been robbed systematically and continuously by a woman working there as a housekeeper, Rosa, with the help of Kippy, eventually caught the thief red-handed. A newspaper reported the case when Rosa was subpoenaed as a witness for the prosecution:

'Dog finds woman crouching in corner of Hotel.

'"The more I shook her the more things fell out," declared Rosa Lewis of the Cavendish Hotel, Jermyn Street, giving evidence today. The woman, charged with stealing silk stockings, bottles of stout, port and other articles, was Marie Turner, who had been an assistant housekeeper in the hotel.

'"She had taken things from every room she had been in," said the proprietress. "The dog showed me where she was crouching in a dark corner of the passage; she was trying to get out of a side door."

'Magistrate: "Was she 'shedding' as you describe it, a cigarette-case and other articles?"

' "Yes, I found the things on her." '

Rosa once brought a case against an American family who left the hotel without paying their bill in full, claiming they had to leave because of the noise that went on all night in other rooms. At that time a charming old woman named Lady Wilson was also staying at the Cavendish. She bore witness for Rosa saying that she had always found the hotel very quiet and restful. Rosa won her case, for judge and jury did not realize that Lady Wilson was stone deaf. After this Rosa always referred to her as 'my mascot'.

Through the pink and white marble of Rosa's character ran a red vein of anarchy. She could not bear having to conform to rules and regulations of any kind. Since she always looked upon her hotel as her house, she did not see why she shouldn't serve drinks in it where and when she chose. Edith, on the other hand, was always very strict about keeping within the licensing hours.

But although Rosa frequently broke these laws, she was only once prosecuted – at the beginning of the last war, when she was fined £40, with twelve guineas costs. Mr Walter Frampton acted for her and in her defence said that during the thirty-nine years she had been a licensee no complaint had been made against her. The Cavendish had a wonderful reputation, he argued, and no one contradicted him.

This 'wonderful reputation' might have been sullied had it been known that Rosa sometimes had an urge, in the early hours of the morning, for 'a little gamble'. She would then sleepily unroll a moth-eaten roulette cloth. Shane Leslie, who used to attend these sessions, once received a hint of an impend-

ing police raid. He therefore warned Rosa, but her only reaction was to send a message to the Commissioner of Police.
'Tell him to come here himself,' she said. 'He'll find his signed
photograph hanging in my gallery.' The raid was laughed off.

In 1926 Rosa had conducted her own case when Captain
John William Warren of the Indian Army Reserve of Officers
sued her for the return of clothes and property which, he said,
she was holding. The captain and a fellow officer named
Leahy had rented a flat adjoining the Cavendish, 19 Duke
Street (which had once belonged to Sir William Eden), for
which Rosa charged them a rent of £7. 7s. 0d. a week. There
seems to have been some trouble concerning the accounts
between the two officers for they insisted on being given
separate weekly bills. This was a great nuisance to Rosa, who
didn't hold with a lot of book-keeping and putting things
down in black and white.

On February 6th Captain Warren was presented with his
week's bill for £4. 13s. 8d. (presumably for drinks etc. in the
hotel). By February 13th it had mounted to £9. 7s. 9d. Two
days later the captain said that two men had broken into his
room and seized all his effects, and that evening he received
another bill for £10. 19s. 3d. At the same time Rosa informed
him that he was to leave the hotel but refused to return his
belongings. He then offered to pay the sum owing if Rosa
would return his confiscated property, but she would not
accept a cheque.

In court she explained that she had only agreed to these
officers taking her flat for a short time because they seemed to be
hard-up and 'wished to sell their carpets' (were they rug-ped-
lars on the side?). But the jury ruled that Captain Warren was
entitled to have his property restored, and for its detention he
was awarded £5.

There were other occasions when Rosa resorted to seizure of her clients' luggage, for many of them persistently ignored her bills. I knew a very attractive young ne'er-do-well, who made a rule of avoiding paying all debts until forced to do so. He was extremely good-looking and lived on his charm, which was beginning to wear a bit thin with Rosa for he had been staying at the hotel much too long for her liking. At last she decided that he must go: 'Young A— is the biggest sponge in London,' she said. 'I won't have him hanging around soaking up all those drinks and never paying a penny. He's got all those fancy suits upstairs and I'll take them to settle his bill.'

A was warned of Rosa's intention by a girl-friend and was therefore able to draw up a plan of his own to foil it. Luckily he was on very good terms with his tailor, whose bill was the only one he was in the habit of paying, and had no difficulty in persuading him to act as an accomplice. His role was to wait in the street below while A lowered his suits down to him, one by one, on coat-hangers and then, when the coast was clear, carry them to his shop, only a few doors away, and store them until A could find another nest in which to play the cuckoo.

When Rosa made her raid on the room, the wardrobe was empty and A had decamped.

Not only did Rosa sometimes claim the effects of her debtors but there were occasions when they themselves were pressed bodily into some service in the hotel – not that this was any great hardship, for they still remained 'in the family'.

Commander Crabb,† the frogman, whose death still remains an unsolved mystery, was one of these. He came to the Cavendish to celebrate on a small legacy. Being exceedingly popular as well as very generous, he found all too soon that he had spent

---

† Last seen diving in the vicinity of the Russian flagship *Sverdlot* when the Soviet Squadron visited Portsmouth.

every penny of his inheritance, and was still left with a heavy bill to pay. In order to discharge this debt, he worked in the hotel for some time as an extra porter.

I remember being very intrigued by another of these 'gentlemen porters' – a one-legged dandy in a curly-brimmed grey bowler and a well-cut black and white check suit. What surprised me most of all was his choice of an opening conversational gambit. 'Have you been to any good hunt-balls?' he inquired.

In 1925, when Mary Lawton's *Queen of Cooks and some Kings* appeared in America, Rosa repudiated it and threatened to bring a law-suit there. The book was never published in England. On February 24th, 1925, the following appeared in the *Daily Mail*:

> ### World-Famous Cook
> #### Mrs Rosa Lewis and a U.S. book
> #### 'A Travesty'
>
> '*The Queen of Cooks – And some Kings*:
>
> 'The story of Rosa Lewis, Cook Extraordinary and Friend to the Royalty and Aristocracy of Europe.
>
> 'A literary turmoil which may be taken to the law courts of the United States for settlement has been caused by the publication in America of a book with the above title, and the prompt and emphatic repudiation of its contents by the woman whose life story it purports to describe. The woman is Mrs Rosa Lewis, the proprietress of the Cavendish Hotel, Jermyn Street, S.W.1., who began to earn her livelihood at the age of 12 and won world-wide fame as a cook, sought after by royalty and Society to prepare dinners.
>
> 'The book is the work of Miss Mary Lawton, a New York

journalist, who has presented it as a personal narrative of memoirs related to her by Mrs Lewis and taken down by a stenographer. In a foreword by the authoress, to prove authenticity, she states that when the transcript of the short-hand note was submitted, Mrs Lewis left judgement to be pronounced on it by her servant, Miss Edith Jeffery, who expressed approval on behalf of her mistress. Miss Jeffery denies that she was consulted.

'*A Travesty*.

'The rejection by Mrs Lewis of the 60,000 words of tittle-tattle regarding people still alive and comment on the morals of present-day Society and celebrities which have been put into her mouth is contained in the following statement by her to a *Daily Mail* reporter.

'"The book is a travesty. Miss Lawton on her arrival from America sought to obtain information from me and my staff.

'"One day I took compassion on her and gave a few harmless facts for the purpose of a short magazine article.

'"I learned that while I was on a visit to Norway, typists, book-keepers and personal servants who had been in my service were approached by her, and well known Americans, who are among my friends, were canvassed extensively.

'"Numerous cables of protest against the preparation of a book in such circumstances were sent to the publishers and Miss Lawton, but they were disregarded. I received a cheque and immediately returned it."'

When the book appeared in America it quickly ran into several editions, but the mere mention of it was anathema to Rosa. With difficulty I recently obtained a copy which I read with great interest. I feel that Mary Lawton may have been hardly treated when Rosa repudiated all that was in the book, for, apart from the 'tittle-tattle', I recognize some authentic plums from her repertoire, but they were served in what might be compared to 'hasty pudding'; a pudding which collapsed in a shapeless heap when it was turned out of the bowl.

In 1935 the Cavendish was mentioned in a law-suit when Lord Revelstoke was sued for breach of promise by Angela Joyce (*née* Ivy Dawkins and a former 'Miss England') whom he met by chance in Rosa's parlour. He had since made a happy and suitable marriage and Rosa, being fond of his wife, was most indignant that a chance acquaintanceship formed in her hotel should have caused so much trouble.

The case made front-page news and embarrassing letters were read in court from 'Teedles' to 'Boodles' and vice versa. But Lord Revelstoke won, and Rosa gave a party to celebrate the victory and offered Lady Revelstoke the choice of any evening dress she liked from one of the best French dress-makers, for she felt that the good name of the Cavendish had also been vindicated.

Chapter Eighteen

Huntin', shootin' and fishin' were hall-marks of gentility and masculinity to Rosa. The 'nobs' she had read about when she was a little servant-girl at Myrtle Villas were all sportsmen; Sir William Eden, Lord Ribblesdale and Willie Low were cast in this mould. The walls of the Cavendish were hung with prints of cock-fighting, steeple-chasing and coaching.

How I envied a certain series, which I think was called 'The Fox Hunter's Dream'. In this the foxes were the hunters. Elegant, mincing vixens in green and blue side-saddle habits, top-hatted and veiled, were mounted on hounds, as were the dandy dog-foxes smoking cigars in a lah-di-dah fashion riding straight at their fences after their quarry – *man!* One of these prints depicted a tired huntsman, asleep in front of the fire, dreaming of a corps of ballet-girl vixens.

Rosa's collection of cock-fighting prints was presented over and over again to American couples as souvenirs of their visit to the hotel. 'I'll pack them up and they'll be there just as soon as you get back,' she would say, but they never left the Cavendish.

It is not surprising to find the name of that veteran sportsman, Sir Claude Champion de Crespigny, recurring in her commonplace books. Like Sir William Eden, he believed in keeping up a high standard of physical fitness through boxing. Both these baronets were fiery-tempered but Sir Claude always preferred to settle an argument with bare fists. In his memoirs, *Forty Years of a Sportsman's Life*, he says, 'Every man ought to have some idea of how to defend himself with his bare fists, and above all how to defend ladies who may be in his company and for whose safety he is responsible.'

But his celerity in raising his dadders sometimes led to trouble and there were occasions when he was summoned for assault.

A hansom cab driver, incensed with a sixpenny tip, once unwisely laid his hand upon Sir Claude's collar, who quickly spun his assailant round and squared up to him. As they were laying into each other a police constable appeared. Both the cabby and Sir Claude were summoned to appear at Westminster Police Court.

Another time, when supping at a restaurant, he complained vigorously that the lobster he had been served was not fresh. The waiter retreated from the storm of abuse into the kitchen, but Sir Claude followed him and held the offending crustacean under his nose, whereupon he retaliated by flinging the contents of the pepper-pot in the baronet's face. According to Sir Claude's memoirs, 'the waiter was chastised', but next day he himself had to answer a charge of assault at Marylebone Police Court, where he was ordered to pay a small fine. For some time afterwards his friends greeted him saying: 'What a strong smell of pepper!'

These outbreaks of violence were not caused by alcohol, for he only drank wine and occasionally a glass or two of port.

There were few branches of sport in which he did not excel. He was the first to cross the North Sea in a balloon, having broken both legs on a previous attempt. When he swam the Nile rapids he dived in among the crocodiles. As a horseman he was remarkable, particularly as an amateur steeplechase rider. In 1880, mounted on Brown Tommy, in the Essex Hunt Cup at Colchester, he fell twice but won the race. Although he was said to be 'a mad rider' he always walked round the course examining the ground carefully before he rode in a race. He often competed with Bay Middleton, but said in his memoirs that this famous horseman had one bad fault: 'he spurred his horse in the shoulder, being apparently unable to sit a horse without turning his toes out.'

In 1914 Sir Claude rode his last steeplechase, at the age of 67, but nine years later he was still driving, motoring and sailing.

He was a relative of my father's and I looked upon him with awe when I was a little girl, partly because I was told that he encouraged his two grown-up sons who were nicknamed 'Creepy' and 'Crawly', to settle any disputes in front of him with their bare knuckles, but most particularly because I had heard in the nursery that when he was a sheriff he had exercised his prerogative of hanging a condemned man.

Perhaps Rosa admired equestrianism more than any other prowess in the field of sport. At the Cavendish, Leicestershire mud, gathered out hunting with the Quorn and Cottesmore, was brushed reverently from pink coats, and hunting boots were boned and polished, taking precedence over other footwear. Jevington was a popular meet with the local hunt, with Rosa welcoming the field with warming stirrup-cups and plum-cake.

One of the most privileged onlookers of the Cavendish scene was Shane Leslie, a nephew of Lady Randolph Churchill's and a cousin of Sir Winston's. Whenever he wished to stay in the hotel he was Rosa's guest. He is one of the few writers who were able to work there undisturbed, as he proved in his book *George IV*. When Rosa presented him with some preposterous bill for items he had never ordered, he retaliated by concocting an equally ridiculous mock account for services he had rendered to Rosa and her clientele:

Item: Taking out two American bores (female).

Item: Mending the W.C. in top attic.

Item: Accompanying Mrs Lewis in gipsy dress to a society wedding at the Brompton Oratory, etc.

As his tall saffron-kilted figure, unchanging through the years, swung through the double doors of the Cavendish, Rosa would hurry to greet him; and she even forgave him for being a writer and 'putting her in a book'. In *The Anglo-Catholic* she appears as Louisa who, when introducing people staying in her hotel (the Sackville), is described as 'rinsing them like a sauce through the duller guests'.† This was very much Rosa's method: to stir up all the human ingredients that came to hand, just to see what kind of dish would come out of the mixture.

But although she liked to experiment with her guests it was unwise to try and foist anyone on her who did not conform to her criteria of acceptability, which required that a person should either be aristocratic, American or affluent. Anyone blessed with these three A's received V.I.P. treatment at the Cavendish.

I myself found out how difficult she could be when I tried to persuade her to be nicer to my friend Doris Delavigne, who had none of the A's on which to climb into Rosa's esteem.

Doris first appeared at Maidenhead like a Tintoretto sunrise reflected in the quiet waters of the Thames. Hers were the prettiest legs that ever stepped into a punt or danced a fox-trot at Skindles. She had hair the colour of ripe corn and a flower-petal complexion. Deep-set blue eyes were fringed with enormously long dark lashes. Although her features were far from perfect, they were infinitely more intriguing than those of most classical beauties. Her nose had a fascinating little furrow at the tip and flaring nostrils; her lips were mobile and

† Shane Leslie, *The Anglo-Catholic*.

quivered as she spoke, disclosing very white, slightly prominent teeth with a small space between the two front ones. 'Wouldn't have them changed for anything, darling, shows I'm lucky and sexy . . . and *how*!' she would say, with a hoot of raucous laughter as she sat curled up on a sofa stroking her gazelle-like ankles.

With such fabulously beautiful legs and a small-boned voluptuous body, she looked her best in a bathing-dress or in shorts, and wore these garments whenever she could. She had great taste in clothes and soon decided that her legs were worthy of a new pair of silk stockings every day; these came from Paris and cost a guinea a pair. When she was first noticed in London she was known as 'the girl with the gloves' since she made a habit of wearing, in the evening, long white or black gloves of the finest suede.

She never forgot old friends, and would give almost unworn clothes from expensive shops to less fortunate girls whom she had known in the bright spots of Maidenhead and Henley. She loved jewellery and collected, sold, pawned and gave away what might have been a Maharanee's dowry. One of her early nicknames was 'Miss Goldsmith and Silversmith'. In sealing a promise she would touch her forehead, breast and, in quick succession, her two collar-bones, as she muttered: 'tiara, brooch, clip, clip'.

Although she had the colouring of an English rose, this was a wild rose with considerable temperament and thorns which could draw blood. When she was roused her language was as unrestrained as her generosity; and on this ground Rosa and Doris met at level weights, although the timbre of the latter's voice was more penetrating.

Rosa had noticed Doris Delavigne's legs tripping in and out of the Cavendish. She was a friend of Laddie Sanford's, who played polo for America in the thirties, and whenever Robin Wilson or Jock Whitney gave parties, Doris and her friends Gertie Lawrence and beautiful Barbara Hamilton (who seemed like an incarnation of Emma Hamilton in her youth) were asked. But Rosa summed up Miss Delavigne by saying: 'Young Doris may go far on those legs of hers but, mark my words, she doesn't know how to make a man comfortable.'

There were many men in Doris Delavigne's life, and most of them were rich. But as soon as she met Lord Castlerosse, she set her cap at him with marriage and a coronet firmly fixed in her mind. Their tempestuous love affair, which continued for several years, was like a trip on the giant coaster. (It has been well described in Leonard Moseley's book on Castlerosse.)

When these two came into a restaurant, all eyes followed them. He was so vast that his huge body had difficulty in squeezing past the tables, while she looked ethereal beside him, giving a shining impression of white and gold. She might have stepped out of one of those velvet-lined pink jewel-cases from Cartier which were so often delivered at her house in Deanery Street.

The tables at which they sat always became the focus of interest, because invariably when they dined together they quarrelled; Doris's voice would be raised and her Thames bargee language shrilled round the restaurant. She looked her most beautiful when her cheeks were flushed in temper.

Castlerosse was just as extravagant as Doris. Here was a man who really 'lived like a lord' according to popular conception. 'What's the good of being a viscount if you can't live on credit?' he asked. He was always immaculately groomed and spent a fortune on his clothes, sporting evening suits made of dark inky-blue vicuna, jewel-coloured velvet smoking-jackets, gold embroidered and coroneted slippers, acres of white piqué waistcoats. His heavy satin cravats were stuck with a large pear-shaped pearl tie-pin; one of his overcoats was lined with sable, while another had a collar of astrakhan; in the corner of his mouth there was always a big cigar.

Castlerosse grew larger and larger as he grew older; he had a gargantuan appetite and could drink like a Titan gulping down the tide. To this colossal presence was allied great wit; his latest *mots* were always repeated round the town and his column in the *Sunday Express* had a sparkle and personality that have never been achieved since.

But Rosa was right, for when Doris married this lovable, impulsive, impossible man she did not make him 'comfortable', since he was always tormented with jealousy on her account. Yet in spite of the violence and frequency of their quarrels they had equally violent reconciliations, for they could do neither with nor without each other.

They quarrelled in public as much as in private, and during these scenes they looked like figures from some unknown fable by Aesop: a virulent blonde shrew-mouse goading an elephant until he careered through the jungle of café society in a state of purple must. Doris knew just where and how to needle Valentine: by wearing a new piece of jewellery and refusing to tell him who had given it to her, by making fun of his appearance, mocking him as a lover.

She would drive him into a state of frenzy over the telephone, as I once witnessed at a restaurant called Josef's, in Paris, where Henry and I were dining with Lord Beaverbrook, whose guests we were on a yachting trip up the Seine. At this time our host was going through a phase of eating nothing but roast chicken (I am thankful to say that this is now past) and I was close to tears, snivelling over the inevitable fowl as I caught pungent whiffs of garlic, my mouth watering at the sight of other lucky people eating snails, *truffes sous la cendre*, and *canard à l'orange*. Instead of this frustration making Valentine lachrymose like me, it only made him increasingly irascible, and in this mood his thoughts inevitably turned towards Doris. What was she doing at that very moment? Muttering that he had to telephone, he heaved his enormous bulk out of his chair and, stampeding over Henry, as though he was an obstructive sapling, lumbered towards the telephone box and put through a call to London. The conversation lasted only a few moments. It ended with a shrill trumpet of rage, followed by the telephone receiver being flung into the restaurant in a tangle of uprooted wires.

As a postscript to this I must add that some years later, on going back to Josef's, Lord Beaverbrook was greeted by the owner as 'Lord Castlerosse'. When he denied this identity, the perplexed patron said, 'But surely Lord Beaverbrook is the very big gentleman who was with you the last time you came?'

'What makes you think so?' Max inquired.

'Because the very big gentleman said, "Put the call to London and the damage to the telephone down on my bill. I'm Lord Beaverbrook."'

But Doris was likewise jealous of Castlerosse and accused him of love affairs with his many women friends, even when the relationship was purely platonic. She made outrageous scenes which often ended in physical violence, with her telephoning to her lawyer and summoning the Phantom Rolls to drive her off and have her bruises photographed for divorce evidence. Next day, these marital battle-scars would be exhibited to all her friends over pre-luncheon drinks in the palm-court of the Ritz. She even managed to carry off a black eye with a certain *brio* and was always supported by loyal women friends.

This tormented couple separated many times, but invariably patched up the quarrel after a term of separation. Castlerosse's 'Londoner's Log' in the *Sunday Express* was the barometer which showed the tempo of their disruptive life together. On the rare occasions when it was running smoothly, he would write lyrically of women, but this phase never lasted for long and soon he would be licking his wounds, flaying the female sex in print, attacking in particular his wife's allies.

Doris's endearingly frank confidences, her determination to make people like and accept her, won her many friends. She was kind to older people and bridled her tongue and tempered her conversation in their presence. When she came to stay at Long-leat for a week-end party which my father-in-law allowed Henry and me to give there, she sat next to him at dinner one night and carried on an animated conversation with him on the subject of County Councils and hospital management, charming him completely.

Winston Churchill admired her both for her beauty and forthrightness. He painted a portrait of her,† at Maxine Elliot's villa in the South of France, in which her fabled legs, clad in shorts, are shown in all their glory.

Although Doris was no blue-stocking, she had many intellectual friends. Lord Berners was particularly fond of her and she often used to stay with him at Faringdon. 'Let's dish the dirt,' she would say as she curled up on a sofa; and Gerald Berners, sitting at the piano, would listen fascinated to her tales of rascality and violence, striking an occasional chord and making some Puckish suggestion for a happy solution to her marital dramas such as putting an announcement in *The*

† Now in the possession of the Marquess of Bath.

Times saying that Lady Castlerosse and Lord Berners were leaving the Isle of Man for the Isle of Lesbos.

Doris was perhaps over-anxious to be liked and received in conventional circles, but could never sense when she happened to make a bad impression. Rosa, for instance, who did not know her very well, always insisted on treating her with haughty disdain. Hoping to improve the relationship between them, I arranged for them to meet over a quiet drink at the Cavendish. From the very start I realized this meeting was unfortunate, to say the least. The atmosphere was charged with Rosa's smouldering hostility, and her eyes widened in a steel-blue stare as they fixed on Doris's stripes of diamond bracelets. 'You should write a book and call it "Round the world in eighty beds",' she said. 'I don't like diamonds ... rather have my yaller beads.'

Rosa did in fact possess some very beautiful diamonds given to her by Sir Coleridge Kennard, who was for many years an *habitué* of the hotel. One of his gifts was the brooch made in the design of a shooting-star, another was a lovely Napoleonic bee.

This aesthetic man, who looked as if he were carved from ivory, worshipped beauty and wrote strange exotic books which read like prose versions of Omar Khayyám. (One of them was dedicated to Max Beerbohm.) Formerly in the diplomatic service, he was at one time Minister at Teheran.

Rosa was devoted to him and when he was staying at the Cavendish he was one of her prize exhibits. She would try to make him join in all the junketing but although he obeyed her summons, he always remained in the background, an amused and inscrutable observer.

Rosa's attitude towards people like Doris Castlerosse, who had climbed the social ladder, was usually one of hostility, yet she was proud of the depths from which she herself had ascended. On the other hand, she had infinite compassion for those who had foundered in an unequal battle against the turbulent currents of life.

I do not believe that Americans ever suffered from this hostility of hers which at times was only too apparent. Their nationality alone was enough to put them in her good books, although she had a distinct preference for the older and richer families such as the Mellons. Theirs was the sort of background that she admired and understood – hunting with liveried servants, shooting luncheons in marquees specially raised for the day, field-trials held on broad acres, and champion dogs with long distinguished pedigrees.

Mrs Richard Mellon, to whom Rosa subsequently gave one of Kippy's descendants (thus perpetuating, to her great pride, the Cavendish strain in America), always came to see her when she was visiting England. One day, on arriving, she found her standing on the steps of the Cavendish, waving good-bye to three other Americans – Bob Coe† and his brother Bill and sister-in-law Clover. Rosa had known Bob ever since his Oxford days, but this was the first time she had met these other members of his family. They had been entertained royally with a jeroboam of the best champagne, and Rosa was in bubbling spirits although a trifle confused. 'You've got to come back and see Mrs Mellon,' she bawled down Jermyn Street after the retreating figures, who obediently returned. On the steps of the hotel she then introduced them: 'This is Mrs Coe with her two drunken husbands.'

Not every American was as rich as Rosa hoped or supposed. When Alexander Sedgwick of Connecticut, for instance, turned up at the Cavendish in the early twenties on the last lap

† Hon. Robert Coe, a former American Ambassador to Denmark.

of a European bicycle tour, his finances were at a very low ebb. He had been advised to call on Rosa by his father, who held affectionate memories of her for he had volunteered as an ambulance driver in the 1914 War and on Armistice night was actually staying at the Cavendish which, he told his son, he associated 'with the last joys of my fleeting youth'.

Young Shan found Rosa in her parlour which was full of people drinking, and introduced himself. She made a great fuss of him and as a mark of her esteem filled a big silver loving-cup with champagne. By the time it was finished everyone else had slipped away and he was left to pay the bill. He did so with pride, although it was the largest single item of expenditure on the whole tour.

Chapter Nineteen

The summer of 1939 shone with a halycon light. Never in my memory had there been so many balls given on a grand scale in London. The atmosphere was tense and feverish, no one dared to pause and the music went round and around. At Blenheim, where a coming-out dance was given in July for the Duke of Marlborough's daughter, Sarah, thoughts turned involuntarily to that other ball given by the Duchess of Richmond on the eve of Waterloo.

When the war began I thought I would not see my friends until it was all over. Living as I did in Wiltshire, with our house turned into a home for crippled children, I expected never to go to London, but after the first few months it was difficult to keep away, and since the countryside round Bristol was being heavily bombed and the black-out was everywhere, it was easier to face such trials at the Cavendish and among friends.

With the years, the hotel had become increasingly dilapidated; it seemed to be ageing with Rosa. The old American clientele still remained faithful, but no newcomers were in evidence. The Cavendish could no longer be called comfortable. You might open a cupboard and find an old polo-stick, a solar topee or a parasol. You had to run the bath water for so long before it got hot that the pipes might have been laid as far away as Southampton, and the telephone was apt to get switched through to your room and remain so until you were driven almost crazy by the spate of incoming calls. The service was either very old and creaky, or of the 'Can I do you now?'

variety; bells were never answered, and you had to raid the pantry (which for some unknown reason was called the dispensary) to get a drink.

With conscription in force, it was becoming more and more difficult to get servants and Rosa's one stand-by was Charles Ingram, who had been with her for many years, and had become a sort of general factotum. Hunted, harried and teased by her, he bore everything with amused tolerance, but when his call-up papers came he was ready to go. Rosa was dismayed and promptly sent him round in person to Downing Street with a note for Winston Churchill. He was shown in to the Prime Minister's private secretary, who, after reading the letter through, asked him if he knew the contents. No, he didn't.

'Don't you really want to join up?' asked the private secretary.

'Oh Lor' yes!' he replied, shaking with agitation. '*Do* ask Mr Churchill to let me go to the war.'

But Charles, who anyway suffered from ill health, did not go and remained at Rosa's side throughout the bombing.

The 1914 War was engraved on Rosa's heart in characters of fire which had cicatrized her feelings, preventing her from mourning overmuch the loss of loved ones of the present generation. With age had come a slowing down of emotion. She was apt to confuse the two wars, talking of the trenches, and of Generals such as French, Kitchener and Haig.

As the Irish Guards had been her favourite regiment in 1914, so in 1940 were the 60th Rifles. Was this because it had been Lord Ribbesdale's old regiment? She took a special pride in his grandson, Lord Lovat, and kept all the cuttings from newspapers reporting his commando exploits.

To the skirl of bagpipes Shimi Lovat led the commando raid against the Germans at Dieppe. (He had caused some considerable damage in a more light-hearted pre-war battle on the French coast, at Le Touquet, when the furniture at the Hermitage Hotel was used as missiles during a Bucks Club week-end.) Before he joined the commandos he was an officer in the Lovat Scouts, a mounted regiment raised by his father. Once when Rosa was in one of her bad moods, which even he could not break through, she said: 'I can't think what's come over young Shimi these days. Those boy scouts of his have gone to his head.' But usually her eyes would brighten when his tall kilted figure swaggered into her parlour filled with photographs of his young Lochinvar gallop through life.

It was very seldom that he could set a foot wrong where she was concerned, but there was one night when she was thoroughly angry with him. This was before the war, when he was a regular soldier in the Scots Guards and he and some brother officers gave a party at the Cavendish. It grew very rough, and again the furniture was hurled around, for one could have applied Hillaire Belloc's words to Shimi:

> 'Like many of the upper class
> He liked the sound of broken glass.'

But, after all, the furniture *had* belonged to his grandfather. When the party was over, Rosa surveyed the damage and her temper soared. Flinging her fur coat over her flannel nightgown and armed with the mangled remains of a piano, she stumped down Birdcage Walk to Wellington Barracks where she bearded the Sergeant of the Guard, demanding the immediate arrest of 'Young Shimi and that scoundrel Dermot Daly'.

He was soon forgiven, for Rosa really enjoyed his parties more than anyone else and saw to it that he never had to foot the bill.

With every hotel in London filled to capacity – most of them so heavily booked that they would not allow their clients to stay for more than two nights – the Cavendish continued to provide accommodation, not by applying the same rules, but by letting two and sometimes three people doss down in a single room. Thus my present husband, Xan Fielding, on a week's home leave after three and a half years spent in enemy-occupied Crete, found himself sharing a room with his friend Rowland Winn.† He must have wished he was back in one of his snug Cretan caves, disguised as a shepherd, with no sartorial problems, for his only pair of trousers vanished when he gave them to Edith to be pressed, and he had to remain in bed until he could borrow another pair.

Patrick Leigh Fermor, likewise on leave in London after kidnapping a German General in Crete, was also drawn to the Cavendish. When he was ill in the hotel, Rosa fussed over him and, in Paddy's words, 'used to sit on my bed and feed me with pheasants full of shot'. Once again she was ready to overlook bills and lend young officers money when they ran short. By way of compensation she would resort to her usual method – not always with success, for the rich who could afford to pay other people's bills were no longer in evidence at the Cavendish.

In spite of the blitz, I found many friends staying with Rosa. At night we all remained in the hotel or dodged out for a quick meal at Quaglino's, Prunier's or one of the Jermyn Street restaurants, for even by war-time standards the food at the Cavendish was the plainest of English. Often we took Rosa with us and her conversation, which was becoming more and more surrealist, always caused a minor sensation. Sometimes I brought pheasants or a haunch of venison from Wiltshire and we would then all eat at a big round table in the dining-room.

† Now Lord St Oswald.

There were jolly nights when we donned fancy-dress and, after the meal, sat singing in chorus until we were hoarse. Rosa's favourite song was 'Two Old Maids Got Locked in the Lavatory'. Sometimes to amuse her, as well as ourselves, we had a cabaret show. Malcolm Munthe, the son of Axel Munthe, who was much loved at the Cavendish where he was nick-named 'Skirts' (because he wore a kilted uniform), used to give his own uninhibited rendering of operas, taking each part in turn and making lightning changes of costume. Being very absent-minded, he was apt to forget later on that he was still dressed as Brunhilde, with hanks of knitting-wool for hair hanging from a tin-pot on his head, and his chest stuffed with cushions, and thus attired would pay romantic and ardent court to a Circe of the Cavendish circle.

Rosa often dropped asleep in the middle of it all and would wake up as the bombs began to fall and the anti-aircraft guns in Hyde Park opened up. 'They're all playing polo,' she would say with a seraphic smile and drop off asleep again.

For a long time this remark puzzled me and it was only after I began writing this book that I realized she was dreaming of her beloved polo boys of the old days, confusing them in her mind with the lively young Americans now staying in the hotel who likewise knew how to enjoy themselves and were up to all kinds of jiggery-pokery.

John Alsop was one of these and came to the Cavendish on leave after parachuting into France. During our impromptu performances he would do turns wearing an assortment of headgear ranging from a bowler hat to a coon-skin cap. His favourite number was 'Dangerous Dan McGrew', which he recited wearing the Davy Crocket cap, emphasizing the words by brandishing a shillelagh acquired in Ireland.

Another, Hod Fuller of Boston, a blue-eyed golden Viking

of a man, sometimes tired of the Cavendish play-pen, and, resplendent in the full-dress uniform of the Marines, used to leave us for more elegant gatherings. It was a source of fascination to both Rosa and me that under all this splendour he had a magnificent fighting-cock tattooed over the broad surface of his back.

Another favourite was Reeve Schli, who looked like a kindly bear in uniform. Rosa was particularly pleased with him because he chose to hunt with the Quorn and Cottesmore during his leave.

Yet another, Jim Fosberg, was a quiet observer of the wartime Cavendish and a frequent recipient of many confidences. His *nom de guerre* in the hotel was 'True Love' since he remained so wise, gentle and philosophical throughout many emotional crises.

When I became Librarian to the American Hospital which was built in the park at Longleat, Rosa always managed to provide rooms for the doctors, nurses and red-cross girls when they came to London on leave. They used to bring her presents from the P.X. and were astonished when the dear sweet old lady they took her for was able to knock back the champagne and brandy with them until they were in no state to know *whose* the bill was.

Of all the Americans who came to the Cavendish, I cannot remember one that was coloured. Indeed the only coloured person of any nationality that I remember seeing there was an Indian Maharajah. Since he was very rich, one of our friends, for Rosa's sake, had invited him in for a drink, hoping to persuade him to move from the Ritz where he was then staying. He was a dark-skinned, tubby young man, who talked very slowly in a sing-song tone. Whenever he spoke to Rosa he raised his voice, enunciating every syllable with exaggerated clarity, addressing her as though she was stone deaf. She must have found this very boring, for she fell asleep in the middle of one of his laboriously perfected sentences, only to wake up a few minutes later, with the embarrassing remark: 'What's that black man doing here? Give him some ink to drink.' The young man smiled blandly and bade her a ceremonious farewell with the words, 'It is very nice to see aged lady who understands the pleasures of youth.'

None of us ever saw him again.

During the war my children continued to stay at the Cavendish on their way back from school. On one of these visits my daughter Caroline, thinking she might feel hungry on the journey, asked Rosa if she might have a packet of sandwiches.

'Of course you can, my dear,' Rosa replied. 'Come with me and we'll see about it.'

Caroline followed her out of her sitting-room into the hall, where an elegant Wren officer sat reading a paper and smoking a cigarette over a gin and tonic.

'Here, you're doing nothing,' Rosa said. 'Go and cut the child some sandwiches – she's Henry and Daphne's daughter.'

'But Mrs Lewis, I'm one of your guests!' laughed the Wren.

'I don't care what you are – a tart for all I know – but you just go and cut the child some sandwiches.'

The Wren officer trotted off meekly to carry out the order, leaving a blushing Caroline assuring Rosa that after all she wasn't really hungry.

Throughout the winter at the Cavendish there were always coal and wood fires blazing in the hall, Rosa's parlour and the Elinor Glyn. In those war-time days when coal was rationed and wood became increasingly difficult to get, the fires had to be cut down. One night there was no fuel to burn, but Rosa, who was always inventive, descended to the cellar and came back with her arms full of boot- and shoe-trees, made for the foot-gear which had belonged to Lord Ribblesdale, Sir William Eden, and other well-shod gentlemen. The flames leaped and crackled as the boxwood burned and Rosa sat in her winged arm-chair in front of the fire warming her old bones.

About this time, Rosa let one of her Duke Street flats to Lord Kimberley, who was Winston Churchill's private secretary. In the twenties, before he succeeded to the title, handsome Jack Wodehouse was renowned as a first-class polo player, and his family and friends used to refer to him as 'The Father of Polo and the Bath', since he was also Chairman of the Bath Club. Here he could always be found playing bridge serenely in a gallery above the swimming pool, impervious to the splashes and shouts of the bodies disporting themelves in the water below. P. G. Wodehouse was his cousin and the character of Bertie Wooster was very probably based on him.

His father was a very eccentric character. After his wife's death he became a recluse, refusing to leave Kimberley or to allow anyone in the place. The park gates were kept locked against all intruders. However, it eventually became urgent for him to go to London to see a specialist. When the day came he started in good time to catch the train, but as he drove through the market-place he looked up at the clock and saw he was early; so he dismissed the chauffeur and walked the rest of the way to the station. When he arrived, the London train was just pulling out. This infuriated him so much that he hurried back to the market-place, seized a turnip off one of the stalls, hurled it with all his might at the face of the town clock and smashed it.

Later in his life, when he became seriously ill, he had to

travel to London once again to see a specialist, for he would not allow even a doctor inside the gates of Kimberley. With the greatest reluctance he agreed to go into a nursing-home where an operation was performed from which there was no hope of his recovering. He had been unconscious for many hours when he came to and saw a beautiful young nurse standing at the foot of his bed. 'Take off your clothes!' he commanded. These were his last words and, having uttered them, he died.

When his executors, shortly afterwards, went up to Kimberley, they discovered the reason he would not allow anyone inside the place: it harboured a seraglio of mistresses and their offspring, all living in perfect amity under the same roof.

Jack Kimberley was in the Duke Street flat when it received a direct hit. He was killed. The same bomb also badly damaged the Cavendish, and Rosa's parlour was wrecked. Shane Leslie, who was a fire-watcher during the war, heard of this at his headquarters and at once went to investigate. This, as he describes in a letter to me, was what he found:

'I made my way down Jermyn Street, which was blocked with rubble and glass. Poor Jack Kimberley had just been carried out of his flat unrecognized. Two peers were killed that night and I dreaded to find Rosa a victim, but found her seated in a chair in her porch being served with cups of tea. Hanging by his hands to a pillar beside her was a good Bishop in gaiters, who had been blown out of St James's Church in Piccadilly. The scene was memorable. "A Bishop in the Cavendish!" I cried. "The day of Judgement must have come."'

Rosa's first words as she surveyed the wreck of her parlour after the bomb hit the hotel were: 'Well ... they didn't get the champagne.' With great difficulty she and Edith were persuaded to leave and go to the Hyde Park Hotel. They were escorted there by Eddie O'Brien, a Cavendish regular, and Rosa's greatest concern was for the hamper of champagne that was loaded on to the taxi. As they were driving off, she popped her head out of the window and shouted to the faithful Charles, 'I want all that mess cleaned up and everything put back straight by Monday.'

She stayed away only two days and no sooner was she back than the Cavendish was hit again. The near-by Hammam Baths were wiped out by a bomb on the same night. In latter years this old-fashioned and opulent establishment had become essential to Rosa's male clientele who depended on its towelly, steaming sanctuary for the amenities unavailable at the hotel. Here they could have their suits pressed, their shoes cleaned, and be barbered and manicured. With the loss of the Hammam Baths went all hope of keeping up outward appearances within the walls of the Cavendish, so that those who lingered there for long henceforth showed a certain lack of physical and sartorial bloom. The raids continued day and night, but she refused point-blank to take refuge in the cellar although she would sometimes go to the air-raid shelter at the Ritz. She remained outwardly unmoved, but the bombing affected her health, and in the last year of the war she became very ill. Finally she had to give in and go to a nursing-home. She must have been utterly impossible as a patient and she stayed there only three weeks. As she was leaving she met Richard Hillary, the author of *The Last Enemy* and one of our most gallant fighter pilots in the Battle of Britain.

'Why . . . I thought you were dead!' she exclaimed, catching hold of his arm with that grip of hers which still retained its strength in spite of her illness.

'Not yet, Rosa,' Hillary replied with a smile.

'Well . . . listen to me,' she said. 'Don't you ever die. I know something about it. In the last two weeks I've been right up to the gates of Heaven and down to the back door of Hell – and they're both bloody.'

Chapter Twenty

When Rosa came out of the nursing-home, she was very frail. She had lost a great deal of weight and the beautiful bone structure of her face was now more apparent than ever. Her vitality was noticeably decreased and she spent a lot of time sleeping. Coming into the dining-room at the Cavendish as she sat dozing with the last rays of the afternoon sun shining down on her white head, one marvelled that such beauty had withstood the onslaught of so much champagne and brandy throughout the years.

Edith was very worried. 'The doctor says she must have a change, dear, but she just won't hear of it. If only we still had Castle Rock or Jevington. I wish they hadn't been sold. She hasn't been anywhere else for over twenty years.'

'Why don't you both come and stay with Henry and me in Wiltshire?' I asked.

'Now that would be lovely. I believe she'd like that, but if we fuss her about it she won't move. I'll have to think it over, dear.'

Edith made discreet preparations for Rosa's visit to us at Sturford Mead. She herself was unable to leave the hotel, but Gladys, the telephonist, was willing to deputize as lady-in-waiting. On the appointed day Henry sent his chauffeur-driven Bentley to fetch us. Rosa had not been told of the plan and both Edith and I half expected that she would dig in her toes and refuse to budge. She was in a good mood after some mellowing midday drinks when I said, 'Rosa, you're like me – you love

189

doing things on the spur of the moment. Henry's sent his car for you. It's waiting outside, so let's drive off to Wiltshire. He wants you to see Longleat.'

To my great surprise she agreed at once.

On the journey down, she sat regally at the back of the car with her lady-in-waiting beside her, and as soon as we arrived at Sturford Mead I settled her into a ground-floor wing.

She might have been a famous film star from the attention the Press gave this visit: the telephone never stopped ringing. My one worry was that she might get bored in the country, isolated from her little realm. It was essential for her to have a complete rest, but it was impossible to keep her in bed for long. Her matutinal habits would not die and Rosa de Bonne-Heure required the earliest of morning tea and scorned the idea of breakfast in bed. Round about midnight she was at her liveliest and the reminiscences began to flow.

'Yes . . . we've had them all to stay: Bishop Potter, he was very particular, not like Professor Pumpelly – and his wife, they used to live all over the world in tents and talk all night about their grandchildren. That man who invented the telephone, and Marconi with all those little bits of fluff – for a joke we rigged up a bell that rang over his head all night. Then there was that comic, what's his name . . . Charlie Chaplin. He was there at the same time as Mrs Al Capone, when Naps Allington was always popping in to say his Alka Seltzer was corked . . . Melba liked the place too . . . the Duke d'Orléans, he got into trouble over her – always liked them fat. . . .

'They say young Peter Wilson – you know, Lord Ribblesdale's grandson – is the best auctioneer they've ever had at Sotheby's. His Lordship would have been proud of him being so artistic, and the other boy, young Martin, he's got an antique shop, with his old butler looking as cross as two sticks sweeping the pavement outside in the Portobello Road.'

And so she would run on, putting off going to bed as long as she could, like a child who hates the dark. I began to feel the strain: the Rose flourished but the Daphne wilted.

The reminiscences continued to flow when I showed her round Longleat and, as so often happens with the old, her memory of the past remained crystal clear although she confused contemporary events and people. Stopping in front of a portrait of Henry's mother, she said, 'She was Violet Mordaunt, wasn't she?' I told her she was quite correct, and illuminatingly for me she opened the gates of her recollection:

'Such a shindy there was over her poor mother's divorce. Only 22 and what a good-looker. Everybody was running after her and then, when young Violet was born, she went barmy. Told her husband it wasn't his baby. She said Lord Coles was the father ... You see, she thought the baby would go blind unless she confessed to her husband about all her carryings on. She gave the names of a whole bunch of the Prince of Wales's friends. Sir William Mordaunt, the dirty tyke, took advantage of this and divorced her. It wasn't fair, with the poor girl out of her mind like that ... Lord Coles, and the Prince of Wales's friend Freddy Johnstone were cited, and the Prince behaved like the real gentleman he was and went into the witness-box. That brute Sir William had gone nosing through all her things when she was ill and found a lot of letters and a Valentine from the Prince. Well ... no letters, no lawyers, and kiss my baby's bottom, as I've always said.'

As we went round the house it was clear she had not lost her discerning eye for furniture since she picked out all the best pieces. When we reached the huge kitchen she looked at the stone floors and sniffed, 'Those poor cooks, standing round on floors like these, it makes my feet hurt to think of it. You've got to be comfortable to cook well, neither too hot nor too cold, that's important. It's cold enough in here to freeze the balls off a brass monkey, and the dining-room seems like a mile or more away. You couldn't serve a really good meal from this kitchen.'

'I bet you could, Rosa,' I said. 'Have you ever had a failure?'

She thought for a moment before replying: 'Not a failure, but I made a bad mistake once. I cooked for a big luncheon on the wrong Saturday, and arrived with it all packed in baskets. It was for ten people. You've got to pay for your mistakes, so I went off to Westminster Bridge and spoke to a friend who had a grocer's stall where poor people did their shopping. I asked him for the names and addresses of customers who hadn't the money to pay their bills, and I gave all the food to these people, and left five shillings in each house as well, just to teach myself a lesson.'

During her visit to us she celebrated her eightieth birthday. We gave a dinner-party in her honour. Before it her hair-dresser and manicurist were summoned from London to attend her. How I should have liked to invite some royal guest to please her! However, she was delighted with the presence of our neighbour, Lady Sybil Phipps, the sister of the Duchess of Gloucester. Rosa, of course, had brought a supply of champagne with her and that night we had Bollinger '21. Henry made a speech proposing her health and we all sang 'Why Were You Born So Beautiful' and 'She's a Jolly Good Fellow'.

Rosa loved looking through the old photograph albums, and whenever she came across pictures of Edwardian figures she usually came out with some revealing forgotten nickname of the time. For instance, my stepmother's family, the Lycett-Greens, who figured prominently in the Tranby-Croft gambling scandal, were the 'Slice-it-Greens', and Berkley-Levett, the young officer in the 10th Hussars who had played poker on the fatal night when Gordon Cummings was accused of cheating, and the Prince of Wales was one of the gamblers, she called 'Baccarat Leverett'. She was well acquainted with the Tranby-Croft case, for at one time she had cooked for Sir Edward Lycett-Green at Treasurer's House, York. She remembered that Lady Warwick (then Lady Brooke), King Edward's favourite for many years, was called Lady Babble-brook because she was reputed to have informed the whole of London of the secrets concerning this disastrous party, known only to the Wilsons, who had tried to hush the matter up.

I took Rosa to see the sights of Bath and we went for drives around the countryside. She showed great interest in everything but I felt she was missing Edith, from whom she had not been separated for more than thirty years. Soon she began to get very restive – a sure sign of returning health – and when the day came for us to motor back to London and the Cavendish she was in fine fettle. This visit had set the seal on her convalescence, she had put on some weight and the roses in her cheeks were blooming again.

Back in the Cavendish, the pattern remained unchanged. She was still followed everywhere by a Kippy – the fourth successor to this name, given to her by one of her fans in the R.A.F. after the third of the dynasty had died. This particular Kippy used a champagne cork for a ball, and on hearing the words 'Doctor Barnardo' would pull a china po from under Rosa's sofa and drag it round the parlour by the handle, barking insistently in front of each person until a coin was dropped in this receptacle. His companion was a grubby white

Pekinese called Kruger, as unsatisfactory as the shares of that name in which Rosa had once invested.

Rosa had always kept her religious faith; this was not obtrusive but remained steadfast in the background. Throughout the years she had been a churchgoer although her attendance was not very regular; I suspect she often went merely to please her clergymen friends. Sometimes she would fasten on one of her clients and march the captive over to St James's Church opposite. 'Does you good,' she would say, as if church-going had the sort of health-giving qualities claimed by Guinness. She would only stay a little while before nipping out, and then return clutching yet another victim she had enlisted at the Cavendish. Sometimes Kippy followed her, pausing to cock a leg on a pew in his progress up the aisle. Once he walked up to the young parson who was reading the lesson, sniffed his feet and wagged his tail as he recognized a friend.

Now on the last stage of her fantastic journey through life, Rosa's faith came out of the shadows. Father Burton, the Bishop of Nassau, always stayed at the Cavendish when he visited London, and on these occasions his laundry was done free of charge – a sure sign of the high esteem in which Rosa held him. Through the years he had become a very close friend and, understanding Rosa as he did, he was able to have long talks with her on the subject of religion. During one of these conversations it emerged that she had never been confirmed. He therefore prepared her for confirmation and himself performed this ceremony. A small dinner-party was given afterwards, and on that night Rosa was armed into the dining-room by the good Bishop himself.

*   *

Although she had become religious, she stuck to her Robin Hood tactics until the very end. Robin McDouall, a client for many years and now the Secretary of the Travellers' Club, after staying at the Cavendish for only two days, was presented with a bill for £16.

'But Rosa! I've only had two gins and tonics,' he protested.

'And think of all the champagne you've had in the past,' she replied.

On another occasion he found Rosa sitting in her chair, in the dining-room, having her afternoon sleep. As he entered, she woke up quickly, as she always did from these light cat-naps, temporarily refreshed and unconfused.

'What do you pay your handy-man?' she asked.

'£7 a week,' Robin answered.

'He'll rob you!' and having delivered this view, she dozed off again.

In 1950 Rosa surprisingly broke her silence concerning culinary matters with a letter to *The Times*.†

CATERING FOR AMERICANS
To the Editor of *The Times*

Sir,

To try to do the impossible and imitate other countries is absurd. Good plain cooking is really the best, and the best requires no trimmings. My idea of plain cooking is that, whenever possible, the article should be cooked when in season and should not be cut up. Let the potato or the truffle stand on its own and be eaten whole. When I visited the United States I found American food outstandingly good but, in my experience, porterhouse steak and roast beef in the United States are underdone and allowed to stand on

† *The Times*, February 7th, 1950.

their own without a lot of trimmings. If we are to entertain Americans in this country we must concentrate on good plain cooking and nothing but the best. They must never be allowed to think that we are trying to offer them the second-rate.

Yours faithfully,

ROSA LEWIS

Cavendish Hotel, 81, Jermyn Street, St James's, S.W.1., Feb. 4.

But despite this the cooking at the Cavendish remained unchanged and such dishes as the game pie described in *Vile Bodies*: 'full of beaks and shot and inexplicable vertebrae', continued to appear on the menu.

In her last days the hotel seemed full of the very young or the very old. Boys like my teen-age sons stayed there and paid only when they had the money. If they were not flush, which was usually the case, the bills were allowed to run on.

After my daughter Caroline married David Somerset, they lived at the Cavendish for several months while they were looking for a house. They had number 43, one of the prettiest suites, with lovely furniture and a little balcony overlooking Jermyn Street. Rosa's memory had by then become more erratic than ever. Everyone was now taken for someone else; the only way to contend with this was to give in and adopt the identity which she had foisted upon you. Although my son-in-law was an established client, she was always muddled as to who he really was. One evening as he returned from the Marlborough Fine Art Gallery where he worked, he met Rosa wandering about in the hall. 'You go on upstairs and see young David Somerset,' she said. 'He's always giving parties.'

Old age brought Rosa no closer to her kith and kin for she

had never enjoyed family life. She had been generous to her parents but saw little of them. She had helped her brothers on several occasions and at one time set one up in a business in Jermyn Street which failed. Another brother came to work in the hotel but left because he said he could not stand his sister's language. There was only one of her relations of whom she was very proud, and that was her sister's son who had delighted her by becoming a captain in the R.F.C. He had an amazing career in the First World War. As a pilot in Arabia he supplied General Allenby and the British Army with aerial photographs – a field in which he was a pioneer. He was in addition an eminent scholar. Dr Hugh Hamshaw Thomas later became Fellow of the Royal Society, Honorary Fellow and sometime Dean of Downing College, Cambridge. He was one of the greatest experts on Botany and Palaeobotany.

There was a dramatic quality about Rosa's looks towards the very end of her life that made me think of tragic figures like King Lear and tired old statesmen who had lived too long. She drifted gently out of this world, dying peacefully at the Cavendish on November 29th, 1952, at the age of 85. A bible and other books of devotion were on the table beside her bed.

Someone – was it Ruskin? – once said that the ideal woman does not gather roses in her path through life, she makes them grow. Though Rosa Lewis may not have been ideal, she was born with this green-finger touch.

Epilogue

There was a mysterious clause in Rosa's will: she left £50 to the Castle Rock 'citadel' of the Salvation Army with instructions that they should play 'God Save the King' on August 5th every year. When the Press questioned Edith as to the meaning of this, she said she thought Mrs Lewis had expressed this wish because she had once been very upset when the Royal Yacht Squadron had not arranged for the National Anthem to be played at the end of a firework display during the Regatta week. She was so indignant that she subsequently engaged a band to ensure that this omission would not occur again. But it is puzzling, since the Cowes Regatta week usually starts on August 8th. Of course she could have easily made a mistake in the date – or did the choice of this particular one commemorate an event which she associated with Edward VII? However it may be, it was typical of her to have carried on her feud with the Royal Yacht Squadron up to the very last ditch.

The remainder of the lease of the Cavendish was left to Edith who continued to run the hotel for ten more twilight years. I never stayed there again, but often dropped in to see Edith; every stick and stone of the place reminded me poignantly of Rosa. Her arm-chair still stood in its usual place in the parlour, with its back to the window, on the right-hand side of the fireplace, but it was usually empty, for no one felt at ease sitting there, and no Kippy lay on the mat in front of the fire. Most of the photographs had been destroyed in the bombing. Only three had survived – Lord Ribblesdale's,

Escoffier's and Father Burton's. These seemed symbolic of the three things which had brought her the greatest happiness in life – Society, cooking and, finally, religion.

In October 1962, poor little Edith had to tear up her roots which had been so firmly planted in the Cavendish for forty happy years. Before she left she had the plaque at the entrance of the hotel removed – it commemorated the spot where the first Kippy had cocked his leg in Jermyn Street every morning – and this was eventually sent to Mrs Mellon in America, who was preserving the Kippy strain.

All the furniture had been left to Edith; she kept what she needed for herself and sold the rest. Most of it was bought privately, for all Rosa's friends wanted some memento of the Cavendish. Sir Philip Dunn bought several pieces and I was at his flat when the enormous chest, which used to stand in the hall of the hotel, was delivered. A gang of men staggered up the stairs with it, just managing to squeeze it through the door. The sight of it brought back a flood of memories, for it was on this chest that the bearskins and tiaras were piled after the Court balls at Buckingham Palace. The rowel marks of spurs could still be seen at ground level on one of its sides, showing where uniformed figures had sat, kicking their heels. Philip Dunn also bought the portraits and prints of the Nelson admirals, as well as the great sofa from the Elinor Glyn, historic as an enormous battlefield . . . how many passionate secrets does it hold?

I went with him to the empty, echoing Cavendish, when he was arranging for the packing of the urns, columns and broken statuary in the courtyard, which he had likewise bought for his house in Wiltshire. I took a last look at the denuded Elinor Glyn, its only adornment the lovely Adam chimney-piece which seemed to have been forgotten. Some of the furniture from here had been sent to America, including a sofa-table and a chair which Rosa had left in her will to Father Burton.

How delighted she would be to know that the lovely baroque mirrors from the hall had been acquired by Oliver Messel to embellish the Assembly Rooms at Bath. But she would have strongly disapproved of the Cavendish's last function, when, after the lease had expired, it was taken by a film company for a few days' shooting of a picture called 'The Party's Over'.

On October 17th, 1962, the following article appeared in the *Evening Standard*:

'The Party is Over'
by Maureen Cleave

'They call this the Kaiser's Suite.† It lies concealed behind a mirror in the passage that turns out to be a door. You would never know it was there. There is a drawing-room, a bed-room and a bathroom. Not many people have been inside. They say the suite was for royal guests only – the royal guests of Rosa Lewis, that fascinating Edwardian beauty who ran the Cavendish Hotel like the mistress of a private house for nearly fifty years.

'Rosa died in 1952. They say it was through the influence of Edward VII that she was established at the Cavendish. She left it to her friend and companion Edith Jeffery, but Miss Jeffery left earlier this year when the lease expired.

'Now the pretty Regency building in Jermyn Street with the little garden in the courtyard is about to be pulled down.

'Already it looks as if nobody cared. The walls are khaki with dirt.

† I had never before heard of a 'Kaiser's suite' in the Cavendish. Perhaps the author was referring to the royal suite used by Edward VII.

'But today the film people who are making "The Party's Over" moved in and did the house a last service – they tarted up the Kaiser's suite. They painted it blue and gold, put tapestries on the walls, carpets on the floors, flowers in the cases and – as the producer told me with feeling – £4,000 worth of furniture in the room.

'The film is about what the director, Guy Hamilton, likes to call "young people who have opted out of Society".

'"Now for this shot we wanted a luxurious hotel. Claridges would have done, but then they would hardly let us pin these lights on the ceiling. Whereas it doesn't matter what we do in this old place. Cost us quite a lot to do it up like this; but I couldn't resist the proportions of this room."

'This evening they move all their stuff out, leaving only the bath in the Kaiser's Suite, which is labelled – fittingly enough – *Shanks Fin de Siècle*.'

A few days later the demolition men moved in to destroy what the *New Statesman* described as 'this mysterious space-time inn at a metaphysical junction'. Let its epitaph be recorded in the words of Rosa's old friend, Sir Shane Leslie:

'Poor Cavendish – I passed the spectral darkened hostelry where Christmas used to be celebrated with all religious and pagan rites.

'The name-plates had been wrenched away like the shoulder-decor of a degraded officer. The windows are like blinded eye sockets curtained by dust. The hospitable doors have clashed for me the last time. Every room has been engaged for Christmas by a ghost. Old crumpled waiters move through the corridors carrying out commissions forgotten in the past. The stairways are thronged but never a creak do they give. The never silent telephone is as dead as Rosa's old heart. With the New Year the last of the Edwardian palaces will tumble into chaos and broken brick and wizened wood and the Cavendish will all be gathered to such as the Mermaid Inn.'

Index

203